£2.77/TP

Libraries in East Africa

LIBRARIES IN EAST AFRICA

EDITED BY
Anna-Britta Wallenius

CONTRIBUTORS:
N. O. Arunsi, S. W. Hockey, C. Kigongo-Bukenya, T. K. Lwanga, P. J. Mhaiki, J. Ndegwa, T. Nilsson, F. O. Pala, J. D. Pearson, S. S. Saith, R. Widstrand, and M. Wise

The Scandinavian Institute of African Studies
UPPSALA 1971

The Scandinavian Institute of African Studies has served at Uppsala since 1962 as a Scandinavian documentation and research centre on African affairs.

The views expressed in its publications are entirely those of the authors and do not necessarily reflect those of the Institute or the institutions where they are engaged at present.

© 1971 Nordiska Afrikainstitutet
All rights reserved
ISBN 91-7106-051-0

Printed in Sweden by
Almqvist & Wiksells Boktryckeri Aktiebolag
Uppsala 1971
ALLF 233 71 001

Contents

1. PREFACE   7
2. LIBRARY SERVICES—FOR WHOM?   9
   Rede Perry-Widstrand
3. THE UNIVERSITY OF NAIROBI LIBRARY   21
   J. Ndegwa
4. THE KENYA NATIONAL LIBRARY SERVICE   31
   F. O. Pala
5. THE LIBRARY OF THE UNIVERSITY OF DAR-ES-SALAAM   43
   M. Wise
6. THE LIBRARY AND ADULT EDUCATION IN TANZANIA: A DISCUSSION   53
   T. Nilsson
7. THE LIBRARY AND ADULT EDUCATION IN TANZANIA: A SURVEY   83
   N. O. Arunsi
8. LIBRARIES ARE ASSETS IN NATIONAL DEVELOPMENT   125
   P. J. Mhaiki
9. THE LIBRARY OF MAKERERE UNIVERSITY   131
   T. K. Lwanga
10. THE PUBLIC LIBRARIES BOARD IN UGANDA   145
    C. Kigongo-Bukenya
11. THE DEVELOPMENT OF LIBRARY SERVICES IN EAST AFRICA   163
    S. W. Hockey
12. THE EAST AFRICAN SCHOOL OF LIBRARIANSHIP: PAST, PRESENT AND FUTURE   171
    S. S. Saith
13. AFRICAN BIBLIOGRAPHY SINCE THE NAIROBI CONFERENCE   189
    J. D. Pearson
14. CONTRIBUTORS   217

Preface

A conference on "Library Work in Africa" was held in Norrköping, Sweden, on 30 and 31 August 1965. The promoters were Mr. Bengt Hjelmqvist, the then Head of the Public Library Section of the Swedish National Board of Education, and Miss Bianca Bianchini, the Municipal Librarian in Norrköping. Experts on libraries and adult education from different sectors of the English-speaking parts of Africa were invited and gave lectures. The papers were presented in a mimeographed booklet, entitled *Library Work in Africa,* which was published by the Scandinavian Institute of African Studies in Uppsala in 1966.

Two earlier conferences constituted the background to the meeting in Norrköping. The first one was held in Copenhagen from 9 to 11 October 1961. It was promoted by Mr. Jørgen Schleimann, the Executive Secretary of the Committee for Afro-Scandinavian Co-operation, and himself a former librarian. The conference was organised in co-operation with the "Association Internationale pour le Développement des Bibliothèques en Afrique".

The second conference was a seminar on "Development and Adult Education in Africa", arranged by the Scandinavian Institute of African Studies and held in Uppsala from 14 to 16 October 1964. Library concerns also were discussed at this meeting, because of the close connection between education and libraries. The papers from the seminar were published in 1965 in *Development and Adult Education in Africa,* a publication edited by Carl Gösta Widstrand.

Interest in libraries and library work in Africa does not seem to have decreased since the conference in Norrköping. Evidence to the contrary is increasing, both in Africa and beyond its borders, not only among people in the library profession but also among those in the many fields served by libraries.

The idea of a collection of papers dealing with the present

situation in the library world in East Africa arose while a professional study tour to East Africa was in the planning stage. At this point an inquiry regarding the possible interest in such a publication was sent to the librarians in Kenya, Tanzania and Uganda and met with a lively response.

In the spring of 1969 the experts who had already expressed their interest were asked to send in their manuscripts. To broaden the contents of the publication, Mr. J. D. Pearson, the Librarian of the School of Oriental and African Studies at the University of London, was asked to contribute a paper on African bibliography.

Publication of these papers has unfortunately been delayed, as some of the contributors have had professional responsibilities which left them with very little time for writing. It is hoped that the publication will be of interest not only to librarians but to all concerned in the development of libraries and library work in Africa.

Uppsala, February 1971.

Anna-Britta Wallenius

Rede Perry-Widstrand

Library Services—for Whom?

While reading the principal contributions to this collection of papers on libraries and library activity in East Africa, it may be useful to keep in mind one of the main recommendations of the UNESCO experts' meeting on the national planning of documentation and library services in Africa. The meeting was held in Kampala, Uganda, in December 1970 and included librarians from Kenya, Uganda and Tanzania. The participants stated that:

Libraries stand ready to reach out to every citizen and in every activity. They have a basic role to play in disseminating information about government programmes and development plans and the *understanding* of these plans. They are the instruments of national unity.[1]

Throughout this book the reader will have an opportunity to examine a wide field of library activities. Perhaps one could then begin by observing some of the social realities related to this statement on libraries.

Lester Asheim, in his book on libraries in developing nations, finds that it is probably safe to say that "library services of all kinds, limited though they may be, are pretty well meeting the demands made of them".[2] This judgement seems to hold true for the library services available in East Africa at the present time.

The main demands come from research workers, expatriates and their families, clerical and commercial employees, civil

[1] *Final Report*. Expert meeting on national planning of documentation and library services in Africa. Kampala, Uganda, 7–15 December 1970. Paris, UNESCO, 1971, p. 24.
[2] Asheim, Lester. *Librarianship in the developing countries*. Urbana, University of Illinois, 1966, p. 51.

servants, teachers and students. Secondary-school students, as well as university students, tend to use library premises as study rooms. However, those who might profit from further education adapted to their needs, such as leaders in the communities, the trade unions, the co-operatives, and the political associations and persons in public office often find that libraries and library adult-education programmes have little to offer. To the 75–80% of the citizens of East Africa who cannot read, libraries and books are not of much importance.

The justification for the expensive buildings which already exist for the use of the literate population must be the expectation of more popular demand in the future. But there will not be a demand for library services from the average East African unless the librarians concern themselves about the fundamental form of the library and question their basic attitudes about library services. It is evident from the Kampala meeting, and from the following contributions, that this concern exists. The form of the public library and its services are my main concerns here, and in the remainder of this discussion.

In East Africa the development of public libraries from early times mirrors the British ideal that libraries should be institutions for the recreation and non-formal education of mainly the middle and the working classes. Elspeth Huxley in 1948 and S.W. Hockey in 1960, both British, wrote the reports which formed the basic development policy. Foreign librarians working in East Africa followed the English pattern of adult library education—mainly allowing those who wished to read books to do so.

Instead of tackling the important questions of literacy and encouraging participation in community and national life through increased knowledge of political processes, librarians tended to assume or take for granted a literate public. They depended mainly on sources of books published in a language that the general public could not read.

The Tanzania National Library stock of Swahili books in 1968 was 5% and only 2 $1/2$% of these were being borrowed. The library can hardly be blamed for omitting books that had not been published, but, as the Assistant Commissioner for

Rural Development, J.M. Rutashobya, pointed out, "the use of the library has not been extended to the people who are literate only in the Swahili language ... many of this 5% of Swahili books are unsuitable for the adult community."[3]

Traditional library training has stressed the technical aspects of library work and has followed the imported patterns and assumptions mentioned above. Accordingly, public libraries have got the public they deserve.

Extending library services to every citizen in East Africa would mean (in mid-1970) reaching out to well above 32 million people. This figure, computed from the Kenya 1969 census, the Tanzanian 1967 census and the Uganda 1969 census, is based on an annual growth rate of 3,3% for Kenya and 3% for Uganda and Tanzania.

The number of those who can read and write probably differs as between the different countries, but it is likely to be not more than 25% of the population in all three. Although figures are not easily available, Uganda's rate of literacy was estimated by the librarians at the UNESCO conference to be 35%. Those who can read and write English are much less numerous.

It is important to observe how government money is being allocated to libraries and literacy programmes under the most recent five-year plans. Uganda, during the second five-year-plan period from 1966 to 1971, plans to allocate Shs 7 534 000 to library expenditure and 11% or Shs 796 000 to the national literacy campaign.[4] The Tanzanian plan assigns five million shillings for the development of library services and allocates Shs 214 000 to the Work-oriented Literacy Project during the

---

[3] Rutashobya, J. M. "Books for the literates: Experience in Tanzania", in Ronald F. Clarke (ed.), *Continuing Literacy: Functional literacy and the provision of continuing reading materials*. Proceedings of the Third Conference of the Adult Education Association of East and Central Africa, Makerere University College, Kampala, Uganda, 1–6 January 1968. Kampala, Milton Obote Foundation, 1968, p. 107.
[4] The Republic of Uganda. *Second Five-Year Plan, 1966/67–1970/71, Supplement of Projects*. Entebbe, The Government Printer, 1969, p. 146.

second five-year-plan period from 1969 to 1974.[5] The Kenyan National Library Service is planned to cost Shs 7 230 000 during the plan years 1970–1974, whereas the programme for eliminating illiteracy in Kenya in 20 years will receive less than half that sum.[6]

It is thus obvious that literacy training is not considered extremely urgent. The libraries' prospective book-borrowers will accordingly be recruited mainly through the school system. Even considering the progress made in primary-school enrolment, the annual increase in population indicates that just under half of the children who reach school age will actually benefit from schooling. This leaves the libraries in the position of continuing or further increasing their services to the educated minority.

The fact that illiteracy will continue to be a factor that librarians will have to live with for years to come indicates a very basic educational role for the public-library movement. It should be closely linked to other cultural and educational efforts, including mass education and literacy campaigns. The UNESCO and many other librarians have recognized and stressed this role, but until recently the possibilities of actually linking library services in this way have not been so apparent.

But librarians tend to shun the question of the newly literate and illiteracy and to withdraw behind a screen of professional arguments. Literacy, they say, is a matter for the specialists and teachers. The specialists and teachers do not agree. They resolved at a conference on continuing literacy in Kampala in 1968 that "it is essential that the artificial distinction between literacy training and other forms of adult education be brought to an end".[7] Unfortunately, no librarians were listed as participants at this conference, at which studies of reading

---

[5] The United Republic of Tanzania. *Tanzania Second Five-Year Plan for Economic and Social Development 1st July, 1969–30th June, 1974*, Vol. 1, General Analysis. Dar-es-Salaam, The Government Printer, 1969, p. 4.

[6] Republic of Kenya. *Development Plan 1970–1974*. Nairobi, The Government Printer, 1969, p. 2.

[7] Clarke, Ronald F., op. cit., p. 155.

habits, book production and distribution were discussed and at which the participants went on to pass a resolution regarding the formation of small village libraries on local initiative.

But what is literacy? The aim of most national educational policies is universal literacy. In the third world the difference is mainly in the time target set for this achievement. The necessity for literacy, the argument runs, lies in the greater understanding which a literate community has of political and constitutional processes and in the general improvement, in its economic development. This can be attained through formal schooling, but, as a stop-gap expedient, mass-literacy campaigns can yield acceptable results. Such campaigns, however, are very costly in terms of the material and the human resources required to carry them out.

The ability to read and write among adults, however, is not necessarily related to political understanding or understanding of constitutional processes and other theoretical matters. These forms of understanding are rather related to the ability to understand a spoken message and the ability to remember facts, arguments and lines of thought. These abilities are often highly developed—astonishingly so—in "illiterate" communities.

Recent theory on adult literacy regards the literacy process as an act of knowing, through which a person is able to analyse the culture which has shaped him and to move toward reflection upon and positive action in his world. A reformulation of the literacy concept to mean the ability to receive and understand information and to take part in discussion is emerging, in part, as a selective and intensive work-oriented approach to literacy. The particular relationship between literacy and improved categories of employment is thus emphasized. With this approach, programmes which have a limited impact on societies could be built into comprehensive programmes for the education and training of rural communities. By a combination of social, cultural and economic education and the improvement of vocational skills, libraries could have a special role to fulfil. They could collect, house, provide and even produce educational material of many kinds.

The creation of this type of library service presents organizational difficulties. Libraries are usually under the Ministries of Education, whereas literacy training most often comes under the various Ministries of National Development. Both in East Africa and in Europe, the ministerial "territorial instinct" is very well developed, and the co-ordination of similar activities is difficult.

The recent trend in modern public libraries has been to create many book and non-book activities, with the library as a centre. A national public-library service should have the necessary contacts with schools and other training centres run by the Ministry of Education, which could be used as rural library centres for the production and provision of material. These centres could also be used for discussion groups in connection with educational programmes broadcast by radio.

Implicit in the more recent concepts of literacy is the opportunity for the librarian to reach out in Swahili and other vernacular languages through radio, television and other media with the contents of books, journals and editorials to aid the process of knowing. Technical achievements in agriculture, such as the "green revolution" and the predetermination of sex in cattle, as well as the achievements of East African historians, poets and authors, are all parts of the literacy process which a citizen needs to enable him to proceed to reflection upon and positive action in his world. One does not need to wait until one can read in order to understand, discuss, debate and reflect. Would not this exposure rather stimulate motivation to learn to read, so that one has the wider choice to pursue one's particular interests?

In co-operation with other adult educators, librarians will have to consider ways and means of best using the existing structures to more effectively use the opportunity the mass media provide. The discussion of this topic which follows later in Mr. Nilsson's article provides some stimulating ideas. Almost all the contributors have recognized that so much of the effort that goes into literacy training is useless, unless people have the means to continue their reading.

Whether literacy is really an important contribution to the lives of people or not depends upon the material that the people read after they become literate. At least half of the literacy problem therefore is what to provide for new literates to read in the transition period while they are building up a vocabulary to the level where they can easily read and enjoy standard literature.[8]

It cannot be said that appropriate literature exists, either in quality or quantity, in East Africa. The publishing houses have produced some titles in Swahili, and a few supplementary readers for use in lower primary classes are available in Swahili and several of the other vernacular languages, but the type of material lacking is simple texts printed in big letters in the vernacular languages, to be used as follow-up reading after the literacy courses have ended.

One answer that suggests itself, as Ronald Benge points out in his book on libraries and social change, is that national or public libraries should themselves undertake either publishing or bookselling or both.[9] Libraries could produce material such as information sheets, discussion follow-ups and material on basic issues—but with a local flavour.

However libraries respond to this opportunity, one of the national library priorities should be to collect all the material of this nature that is being produced by the various government departments, institutions and other agencies, so that it is available for study and comparison for those involved in writing and producing this type of material, and a further priority should be getting this type of material to the readers.

Not only the number of people in East Africa but also where they are living is another challenge to the librarian attempting to reach every citizen. In East Africa as a whole, 94% of the population is in the rural areas. The urban population of Kenya is 8% or approximately 825 000, which is higher than Uganda, with 410 000 or just above 4%. Tanzania has an urban population of 5,7% or approximately 700 000.

With this distribution of the population in mind, it is not surprising that the latest plans for each of the East African

---

[8] Dr. Frank Charles Laubach. Quoted in Benge, Ronald C., *Libraries and cultural change*. London, Bingley, 1970, p. 106.
[9] Benge, op. cit., p. 194.

countries stresses the importance of rural development. The Kenya plan boldly asserts that

The key strategy of this plan is to direct an increasing share of the resources available to the nation towards the rural areas ... The Government believes ... that the people as a whole can participate in the development process.[10]

The Tanzanian policy is very much geared towards self-reliance and the creation of a self-supporting and a surplus-creating rural population. This is not only reflected in President Nyerere's speeches, but also in the Plan:

Rural development is the key both to the achievement of the productive targets in the Plan and the social goal of spreading development to the mass of the people.[11]

The Uganda Plan contains simular statements and, as an example of the general trend, it may be mentioned that during the plan period all 615 of the planned community centres (one for each *gombolola* in the country) will be built. The programme is to provide a point where local communities can gather for various activities, such as adult education, club meetings, cultural events and recreation, and where Government services, such as radio and television, can reach a wider audience than they would otherwise reach.[12]

As with most planning in East Africa, the fulfilment of the plans' targets is difficult, but the main trend is very obvious: concentration on the participation of the rural population. This concentration on the rural population by the governments of East Africa raises a fundamental policy question for the library services too: how should libraries be organized to reach the people? On this question Benge has written as follows:

It may well be that, as far as public libraries are concerned, the British model, which tends to separate libraries from formal education, is a most unsuitable one. The educational function of all types of library is paramount, and Unesco's policies have always recognized this. For example, in some countries the most suitable

[10] Republic of Kenya, op. cit., pp. 146–147.
[11] United Republic of Tanzania, op. cit., pp. 70–71.
[12] The Republic of Uganda, op. cit., pp. 146–148.

public library policy might be to set up libraries in schools, rather than to develop a wholly separate library system.[13]

Benge also discusses the possibility of shock programmes, "where service is extended by a massive campaign to place deposit books in every kind of institution—clubs, trade unions, co-operative centres, community centres, political-party organizations and so on".[14]

This discussion has a direct bearing on Ugandan experience in library development, and it may be worth while here to add some information regarding that experience, which Mr. Kigongo-Bukenya has covered in his contribution to this volume. The first director of the Uganda Service ignored the Hockey Report, made his own survey of the country's needs and at the 1965 East African Library Association conference outlined plans to introduce a library system tailored to the needs of Uganda and not imported from elsewhere. He suggested that each of the gazetted towns would have a small library by June 1966, and that book boxes of 200 volumes each would be available to all institutions and community centres. A mobile library would serve schools, administrative quarters and trade centres. A postal service would be offered to isolated readers. In addition, radio and television would present a library hour for illiterates.[15]

Since these collections could not be adequately controlled and did not measure up to common standards for library service, these efforts were judged uneconomic and wasteful. But, as Benge points out, in some circumstances such "waste" could be justified, on the ground that this is the only way by which the mass of people can be exposed to books.

Should efforts be made to develop properly organized, well-equipped headquarters libraries and then branch libraries and then eventually mobile services, or should energy be devoted to providing services in schools, community centres and so on?

[13] R. Benge, op. cit., p. 190.
[14] Ibid., p. 191.
[15] Serwadda, G.W. "The Development of Library Services in Uganda", *East African Library Association Bulletin*, No. 7 (June, 1966), pp. 27–28.

Or would a combination of these methods work best? The number of trained personnel the service can provide is the essential consideration in answering these questions.

Some idea of the future of the Uganda system may be gathered from the meeting of librarians at the UNESCO conference in Kampala. The participants discussed a plan for Uganda library development which was submitted as a working document by a UNESCO consultant.

Considerable reservations were expressed about the proposals for the separate creation of both a national library and parliamentary library ... the creation of a co-ordinating body, as suggested, would be a step forward, but ... it might perhaps be possible for Uganda to lengthen its stride. If the concepts of separate national, parliamentary, public school and special libraries, inherited from the more developed countries, could be discarded, a much more radical approach to the problem could be adopted. What was required, it was suggested, was a single integrated library service very similar to the organizational structure of educational services found in many countries.[16]

Guidelines for a plan for the development of library services in Uganda were prepared by a working group at the conference. They listed as priorities for development: the setting up of a national planning and co-ordinating body, fighting illiteracy by strengthening the public-library service and intensive staff training at all levels.[17]

The emphasis that most of the contributors to this collection have placed on the training of personnel is to be expected. Mr. Saith, in his paper, has given a clear picture of the history, problems and possible future of library training in East Africa. Well-trained librarians are, of course, the key to the future of library activities. In East Africa they have a special role to play. Attention here has been directed to the opportunities which librarians have to work in the field of extending and continuing literacy, to enlarge services of various kinds to the rural population and to improve the kind of organization needed for these purposes.

[16] Final Report, UNESCO, op. cit., p. 18.
[17] Ibid., p. 20.

In East Africa, libraries could not only be conceived of as town buildings, urban branches and bookmobiles. A library could also be a station on a transistor radio or take other, more flexible forms in order to reach the rural population. A librarian need not only be, as the saying goes, "a passive purveyor of books", but could also be a translator and broadcaster of the contents of books. To villagers, he could even be a secondary-school leaver, with a good ability to read, who arrives by bus to give library reading hours and who hands out expert-approved duplicated material for new readers, summarizing the readings.

It is perhaps naive to suggest that in East Africa librarians, who now have great problems in acquiring funds for books, should include in their budgets expenses for translations and condensations in Swahili and other vernacular languages, production of material for new literates, radio programmers and broadcasts in Swahili and other languages, and bus fares for the library's readers. But perhaps this type of activity, more than any other, would give new life to the basic role which libraries have to play in disseminating information about government programmes and development plans and the understanding of these plans.

The type of library work suggested above calls for a kind of librarian who is not produced by present library training. The existing library school in East Africa produces few librarians and they are all needed in the established library services. The training of librarian-educators of the type mentioned above could be organized within the existing framework of diploma courses in adult education, teacher-training institutes and the library school. Mr. Mhaiki and Mr. Arunsi have made some invigorating suggestions along these lines.

If some of the aims of the existing national-library services are to help to fill the gaps caused by the shortage of schools, and to act as social cement between the educationally privileged and the less privileged, if, indeed, they are considered to be instruments of national unity, now is the time to expand the concept of libraries and library activity in East Africa. Otherwise the greater part of East Africa's citizens will never make any demands on them.

J. Ndegwa

The University of Nairobi Library

Preparations for an institute of higher education started around 1947, when plans were drawn up by the government for the establishment of a technical and commercial institute. Later, the ideas grew into an East African concept of higher technical education, with the culmination in 1951, when a Royal Charter was received for an institution named the "Royal Technical College of East Africa".

With funds from the Colonial Development and Welfare Scheme, the Gandhi Memorial Academy Society and the East African governments, the building of the College started in 1952. Although a few external courses were arranged during this period, it was in April 1956 that the first students were enrolled, the actual number being 215.

Studies carried out in the Royal Technical College were mainly designed to qualify students for entry into universities elsewhere or to lead to professional qualifications. This state of affairs changed in 1961, however, when the College made arrangements with the University of London to enable its students to prepare for and take University of London degree examinations. In the same year the College had its name changed to Royal College and increased its student population to 415.

From then on, development was rapid. In June 1963, the University of East Africa was founded, with the Royal College as one of the constituent colleges, the other two being Makerere University College, Kampala, and University College, Dar-es-Salaam. The next year the College was re-named University College, Nairobi.[1]

[1] On 1 July 1970 the College became the University of Nairobi.

Student numbers have increased rapidly during the last 8 years. From a total of 415 in the 1961–62 session, the student population has now reached over 2 000 during the 1969–70 academic year. Numbers of staff have also increased tremendously.

University College, Nairobi, now has seven faculties and three institutes and expects to start two more faculties in mid-1970. Plans are well advanced for the establishment of the University of Nairobi, of which the College will be the main component.

The College has four campuses, one for the Faculty of Veterinary Science, another for the Biological Sciences and a third for the Medical Faculty. There is also the Main Campus, which contains all the other faculties, except the Institute of Adult Studies, which has a centre of its own outside Nairobi.

University College libraries

The policy of the College regarding library services is against the establishment of faculty or departmental libraries. However, due to the number of campuses that have developed, it is not practical to serve the whole College population from one library.

The College therefore runs a library system, comprising the Gandhi Library in the Main Campus, a veterinary-science library some 9 miles away, a biological-sciences library at the Chiromo Campus, which is 2 miles away, and the beginnings of a medical library at the new Medical Faculty, about 3 miles from the Main Campus. There is also a small library at the Adult Studies Centre and a new education library will be started soon.

The library system is organised and administered centrally, the College Librarian being responsible for the running of all College libraries. All technical services, for example, ordering and acquisition of books, cataloguing, binding, processing, etc., are centralised at the main library. Staff in all College libraries are under the direction of the College Librarian and are posted to different libraries according to requirements.

Library buildings

The Gandhi Library is in a large modern building in the Main Campus in Nairobi. The building, which was completed in 1962, can accommodate 300 000 volumes and 500 readers. At the present time parts of the building are being used by other departments of the College, but it is expected that the entire building will be taken over for library services in the next 12 months. It is estimated that the University of Nairobi will have about 3 150 students in 1972, of which some 2 400 will be taking courses conducted at the Main Campus. It is further estimated that the growth of the numbers of students and staff during the 3 years after this period will continue at the same rate. It is therefore recognised that the capacity of the main library will become inadequate very soon and discussions have been started on the plans for building an extension to the existing building.

A building for the Faculty of Science library was completed and taken over in January 1967. This had been estimated to cater for the needs of the Kabete Campus for a considerable time to come. This estimate did not, however, take into consideration the need for development in other fields, as that Campus has now to house a new Faculty of Agriculture. Funds have now been made available for the extension of this building, so that it can cater for the requirements of the Faculties of Agriculture and Veterinary Science.

The Chiromo Campus houses the Departments of Botany and Zoology of the Faculty of Science, as well as the preclinical departments of the Faculties of Medicine and Veterinary Science, together with the first-year students in the Faculty of Agriculture. The library therefore contains practically all the book stock on the biological sciences held in the University library system. The Biological Sciences library, as it is named, is in a new building opened in May 1969. It can house 20 000 volumes and 120 readers.

At the present time the collections for the Faculty of Medicine (only 2 years old) are in a room at the medical campus near the Kenyatta National Hospital. As a part of the developments of the teaching hospital and the faculty buildings, plans are well ahead for a new building for a National Medical Library, which will serve not only the University but the whole medical profession in the country.

A new building for the Faculty of Education in the Main Campus is nearing completion. Practically the entire ground floor and a part of the basement will be utilised as an education library for the University. The starting of a separate education library may seem contrary to the policy of not having faculty libraries, as mentioned earlier. It was realised, however, that the University education centre would have to assist the general development of educational institutions outside the University. Until another organisation capable of advising on libraries in teacher-training institutions and schools was available, the University libraries would have to play this role. It was felt that a separate education library would fulfil such tasks in a better way than the main library.

Library stocks

As in all other aspects of development in the University Library, as indeed in the whole University College, the growth of library stocks has been very rapid, particularly during the last 8 years. From a total of about 35 000 books, pamphlets, and bound volumes of periodicals in 1962, the stocks in the University libraries have grown to about 100 000 in the year 1969–70. During the last 2 years, funds provided for books and periodicals have doubled and it is expected that next year they will be more than four times what they were 4 years ago. The libraries now take about 1 400 current periodicals, as against a total of 500 (of which 210 were gifts) 10 years ago.

The selection of books for the Library is carried on as a cooperative exercise between faculties, departments and the Library. Funds are allocated for each field of study and faculty members are encouraged to suggest purchases. A large central fund is, however, left to be spent at the discretion of the Librarian. In this way, not only is it ensured that the Library has what it feels should be stocked but the growth of stock is as uniform as possible in all fields.

With the development of new faculties in the University, book stocks and periodicals, particularly in medicine, agriculture and law, will have to be built up at a very fast rate. Considerable funds are being provided for this and total stocks in the University libraries are expected to increase tremendously during the next 2 years.

Special collections

It is the policy of the University Library to have as much as possible of its library stock on open shelves, freely accessible to all users. For various reasons, however, it has been found necessary to organise and administer certain materials of special interest as separate collections. The main groups treated this way are as follows.

(a) *United Nations material.* The University Library is a depository for material issued by the United Nations and the Food and Agricultural Organisation. These collections are organised separately as the United Nations Collection.

(b) *East African material.* The Library is also a legal depository for books, periodicals and newspapers published in Kenya, excluding, unfortunately, government publications. The University Library has an East African Collection, which includes these publications, as well as the publications of other East African governments and other library material on East Africa published elsewhere. It is now the Library's policy to endeavour to acquire all current publications on East Africa.

(c) *Micro-form materials.* A collection of microfilms and microcards is gradually being built up of publications which are not available or are expensive or cumbersome in other forms. This is organised in a separate room, where readers for the material are available. The Library does not have actual collections of gramophone records or tapes, although there are odd items of this nature. It is, however, envisaged that such collections will be started in the not too distant future.

Catalogues and cataloguing

Up to 1968, the library stock was classified by the Universal Decimal Classification, and had two catalogues, the author and the classified catalogue. The bibliographical information given in these card catalogues was extremely brief and it was decided that fuller cataloguing was essential, now that the library stock was growing, and growing at a fast rate. In considering this project, it was recognised that one of the major problems which would face the Library would be shortage of qualified professional staff and that any backing from a centralised cataloguing agency would be of immense assistance.

For this, amongst other reasons, it was decided to change the classification to that of the Library of Congress in Washington and to follow, as much as possible, their cataloguing practices. This would enable the Library to use the Library of Congress catalogue entries and possibly purchase catalogue cards from them. After some initial delay while waiting for publications and cards from the Library of Congress, this scheme went into full swing early in 1969. It was later decided that it would be quicker and easier to use the cataloguing entries from the Library of Congress *National Union Catalogue* rather than to purchase their cards and this is what is now done, using a Xerox 914 copier to produce the cards required.

A dictionary catalogue is now in operation in which all entries (author, title, subject, series, etc.) are interfiled in one sequence. Re-cataloguing of the old stock is continuing at an ever-increasing speed.

A union catalogue is maintained at the Main Library, showing all the publications in the whole University Library system. In addition, each sub-library (the term used for each "satellite" library) has a dictionary catalogue of books in that particular library as well as of books of interest to that campus housed in another library in the University system.

Staff

One of the major problems encountered by the Library is that of the recruitment of professionally qualified personnel. There are only a small number of local qualified librarians and the Library, like other University libraries in the area, has to a great extent to depend on expatriates to fill many of the senior posts. At the present time, of the 10 senior posts in the University Library, only four are filled by Kenyans.

A training scheme has been started, under which local graduates are appointed. After some in-service training, they are sent to library schools abroad (the East African School of Librarianship at Makerere having no post-graduate courses) and are appointed Assistant Librarians on qualifying. Six such trainees have already been appointed. One of them is already in a library school and arrangements are being made to send the others next year. As well as this high-level training, funds are being sought to send library assistants to the School of Librarianship at Makerere to both the 2-year Diploma and 6-month Certificate courses, depending on their educational qualifications.

Senior Library staff are appointed on terms equated with those of the teaching staff, the Librarian being equated to a Professor, the Deputy Librarian to a Senior Lecturer and Assistant Librarians to Lecturers. Posts approved for the fiscal year 1970–71, exclusive of clerical, bindery and photographic staff, are as follows:

- 1 Librarian
- 1 Deputy Librarian
- 2 Senior Assistant Librarians
- 12 Assistant Librarians
- 6 Trainee Assistant Librarians
- 12 Senior Library Assistants
- 33 Library Assistants

Services

The Library is not only the centre of research for staff and students but also gives its services freely to research workers from outside the University. It is also extensively used by government officials, graduates of this and other universities, secondary-school teachers and members of various professional institutions that have special arrangements with the Library. Indeed, although the University Library has not been officially recognised as such, it virtually performs the role of the national reference library.

Due to shortage of staff, the Library has not been able to undertake as much bibliographical work as it would like to. An accessions list, with a separate section of publications on East Africa, is circulated both internally and externally. A periodicals-holdings list is prepared periodically to supplement *Periodicals in East African Libraries: A Union List,* which is at present prepared by the Library of the University of West Virginia in the United States. With the expectation of a larger professional staff, bibliographical activities are expected to increase considerably. It is particularly the intention of the Library to explore the possibility of compiling a national bibliography for Kenya. As the only legal deposit library and the only institution with the staff and resources for this work, it has now become clear that the University Library must undertake this duty as soon as is practicable.

The University Library provides photocopies of articles from periodicals and other documents. A Xerox 914 copying machine is operated for this purpose and photocopies of articles from journals are also obtained from other libraries in East Africa and abroad.

Services to readers in the Library have been minimal in the past, again due to shortage of staff. This situation is now being remedied, so that qualified staff will be available to give reference and other readers the services that are so necessary, particularly with students, who, in most cases, have not used a large library prior to joining the College.

Administration and organisation

As stated before, the Librarian administers the whole library system in the University. He is responsible to the Principal for the proper running of the library service. A Library Committee exists to advise the Librarian and the Academic Board on matters concerning the Library and its services. It is composed of representatives from each faculty and institute and a number of members appointed by the Academic Board, whose Committee it is. The Librarian and Deputy Librarian are members of the Library Committee. The Librarian is also a member of the Academic Board, as well as the College Development and Planning Committee.

Internally, the Library is organised departmentally rather than by subject, except in the case of sub-libraries, which cover one or, in some cases, a group of related subjects. Each section (for example, cataloguing, book circulation, periodicals, acquisitions) is headed by an Assistant Librarian. In some sections there are more than one Assistant Librarian, one of them being in charge. There are plans now to appoint two Senior Assistant Librarians, one to be in charge of all technical services (acquisitions, cataloguing and binding) and the other to be responsible for circulation and reference. At a later date, staff being available, it is hoped that the library may enter the field of subject specialisation.

Bibliography

Royal Technical College of East Africa, Annual Reports and Accounts, 1951 to 1959–60.
Royal College, Nairobi, Annual Reports and Accounts 1960–61 to 1962–63.
University College, Nairobi, Annual Reports 1963–64 to 1968–69.
Royal Technical College, Calendars 1957–58 to 1959–60.
Royal College, Calendars 1959–61 to 1962–63.
University College, Calendars 1963–64 to 1969–70.
Ndegwa, J., The Library of the University College, Nairobi. *SCAUL Newsletter*, 5, 1968.
Pearson, J. D. & Jones, R. (*eds.*), *The Bibliography of Africa: Proceedings of the International Conference on African Bibliography*, Nairobi, December, 1967. Frank Cass, 1970.
Ndegwa, J., Developments in the Library of University College, Nairobi, *East African Library Association Bulletin*, No. 10, October, 1969.

F. O. Pala

The Kenya National Library Service

The Kenya National Library Service was created when the National Assembly passed the Kenya National Library Service Board Act in 1965. This Act came into force on April 1st, 1967, when the present Board was formed. The Board, as stated in the Act, has the following functions: to promote, establish, equip, manage, maintain and develop libraries in Kenya. It must be inserted here that, even though the Board's functions would suggest that there were no libraries in Kenya before the Board was formed, the fact actually is that several libraries of different types did exist but they were either too specialised or too limited in scope to meet the needs of the wider public and schools and hence the Board was created to cater effectively for the wide needs of adult, technical and general education.

Before the 1965 Act

Subscription libraries were known in Kenya long before the formation of the Kenya National Library Service Board and in their day they performed a function which was both desirable and necessary. It is therefore proper that a few words should be said here about them. Among the subscription libraries are well-known names, such as the McMillan Memorial Library (started in 1931), the Desai Memorial Library (started in 1944) in Nairobi and the Seif Bin Salim Public Library and Free Reading Room (started in 1903) in Mombasa. The McMillan Memorial Library was taken over by the Nairobi

City Council in 1962. But, before this time, all the three libraries had the following similar characteristics:

(a) They were privately financed, usually through endowments, small grants from the central government and local authorities, and subscriptions by members.

(b) Membership was restricted either to Asians or Europeans only.

(c) The literature available was mainly in English, in Asiatic languages and to a limited extent in Swahili.

(d) They catered mainly for the towns in which they were situated, although in theory they aimed at serving a wider public. The McMillan Library made some attempts to serve people living in places away from Nairobi, but this was a minor part of its activities. It was only made possible by the insistence of the Carnegie Foundation, which provided funds for the purpose from 1932 to 1960–62.

(e) The bulk of the literature was for reference and recreation.

It will be seen from the above characteristics that the subscription libraries had two main shortcomings:

(a) Their area of influence was confined to three main towns, leaving the bulk of the country without library provision.

(b) They were intended for non-Africans in the first place and Africans were not admitted into them, either until after independence was achieved or just when the political climate began to indicate that the Africans would soon be in power.

The inadequacy of their provision is therefore obvious.

Public-library provision for Africans

Towards and after the end of the second world war, the British Government showed considerable and practical interest in the improvement of African social welfare and education in the then colonies. Consequently, in 1944, the Conference of the

Governors of Uganda, Tanganyika, and Kenya commissioned Mrs. Elspeth Huxley to investigate and to report on book production and library facilities with relevance to Africans in East Africa. In 1945 Mrs. Huxley reported, making the recommendation that a Literature Bureau should be established for the following purposes:

(i) The publication of general and educational books.
(ii) The publication of a popular magazine.
(iii) The promotion and encouragement of African authorship.
(iv) The establishment of lending libraries for Africans.
(v) The development of book distribution.

All these purposes are clearly related, but in this paper I shall only concern myself with libraries and in this respect Mrs. Huxley's recommendations were as follows:

(a) A large central library for each of the three East African territories and,

(b) Branching from (a), regional libraries in various parts of each territory.

Due to shortage of funds, it was not possible to implement the above recommendations and instead the following two cheaper forms of library service were launched:

(a) Book-boxes—boxes of about 200 books, lent to schools, community centres, etc.

(b) A postal service to individuals.

Many schools, community centres and individuals took advantage of these services, but, because expenditure remained at a fairly low level, the original target of reaching most Africans was not achieved until the 1960's, which can be described as the Decade of National Library Services in East Africa.

The 1950's

During this decade, which appears uneventful from the point of view of library development and expansion, many events were going on elsewhere which must have paved the way for the development which took place during the next decade. For instance, in what was then the Gold Coast, a Library Board had been formed to organise and to develop libraries for schools and the public; its motto was "Books to the People". In Jamaica and Trinidad a similar event took place. In all these cases the moves were inspired by the British Government, who provided the initial funds and the know-how. It is important to note here that Great Britain was taking much greater interest in the improvement of education in its widest sense in Africa and, in this connection, many conferences financed by the British Colonial Office, assisted by some private foundations, took place to study the post-war problems of African education and to make suitable recommendations to the various colonial governments. It is particularly worth considering the influence of the Nuffield Foundation Conference, which was held in 1952 on the subject of *Educational Policy and Practice in British Tropical Africa*. In the two parts of the report dealing with West Africa and East and Central Africa, it was made quite clear to the British Government that the demand for education in the African territories was evident and forceful and that educational planning and policy must bear this fact in mind. In the same report a point was made of the need for good library facilities not only for the general public but also for schools, teacher-training colleges and literate adults.

It will be seen therefore that, unlike the 1940's, the 1950's saw a definite policy move on the part of the British Government to implement a new policy on education in Africa— a policy which gave a prominent place to libraries.

The 1960's

In June 1960 the British Council appointed a libraries expert, Mr. S. W. Hockey, as a Libraries Organiser in East Africa. After studying the three territories, Mr. Hockey in 1960 produced a report entitled *The Development of Library Services in East Africa* (elsewhere referred to as the Hockey Report), the gist of which was that a national library board should be created in each of the East African countries and should be invested with the powers to start, expand and develop library services. This plan was accepted simultaneously by each of the three countries, although implementation was quicker in Uganda and Tanganyika than it was in Kenya. Tanzania and Uganda both accepted the recommendations in the Hockey Report and had National Library Boards created in 1964. Kenya's legislature did not pass the Kenya National Library Service Board Act until April 1965 and the Act did not come into force until 7 April 1967, when the present Board was formed.

The Kenya National Library Service Board

The Board is composed of one representative from each of the seven provinces, one member from the Nairobi City Council, one member from University College, Nairobi, and five members representing various ministries, including the Ministry of Natural Resources, which is responsible for library services.

Although the Act came into force in April 1967, it was not until October of that year that the first Chief Librarian was appointed. It can therefore be appreciated that no planned development could begin before the appointment of this officer.

The first five-year development plan

The first job the Chief Librarian had to tackle was to draw up a five-year development plan, which was to be presented to the government and to be incorporated in the national development plan. This was a slow job, as it necessitated visiting all the local authorities, in order to consult them regarding the contribution they would be willing to make towards library development in their areas. This process occupied the months of November and December 1967 and January and

February 1968. The Development Committee of the Board, which had been constituted for this purpose, then sat down to compile the final document, which was later approved during a full meeting of the Board in June 1968. The plan was finally accepted by the Government of Kenya towards the end of 1968.

Area libraries

According to the plan, which covers the period 1969–70 to 1973–74, the Board intends to create five area libraries, to purchase four mobile libraries and to have at least some sort of service for all parts of the country. It is also hoped that a headquarters library will be built in Nairobi to serve as the seat of administration, the orders department, and the cataloguing and classification sections and to provide ordinary library service for areas adjoining the City of Nairobi. It is planned that the headquarters shall include a research collection with a special emphasis on Kenya and Africa. It should be added here that the area libraries will in fact be large regional libraries serving populations varying from about 700 000 to about one and a half millions. The actual library population will, of course, be much smaller, since the rate of literacy is only about 15–20%.

Branch libraries

It is the Board's intention not to embark on the creation of branch libraries until a basic number of area libraries have been constructed and are fully operative. Branch libraries will then be developed in relation with the capability of the area libraries to supervise them and to supply them with books. It is also expected that to some extent the development of branch libraries will depend on the ability and readiness of a particular community to participate in such projects.

Schools library service

The policy of the Kenya Government since independence has emphasized secondary and higher education. Consequently, many secondary schools have recently been started on a self-help basis. Many of these schools are operating on very limited budgets and as a result can hardly afford to make suitable library facilities available. If the effort that has gone into the establishment of these schools is to be utilized for the national advantage, it is important that they should be given adequate book supplies, in order to ensure a good education for their pupils. To do this effectively on a national scale is a massive undertaking, which would require almost as much financial outlay as the ordinary public-library services. It is therefore hoped that the Board will receive financial support from the Ministry of Education for this purpose.

Cost of the plan

To implement this development plan, the Board will need to find at least £340 000 to build a headquarters library and five area libraries and to purchase four mobile libraries. It will also be necessary to allocate not less than £200 000 for books.

In certain quarters these figures will appear rather intimidating, but it is the view of the Board that these sums are the minimum which must be spent if the Board is to establish a worthwhile library service for Kenya. In the meantime the Board will offer limited library service to schools in the form of book-boxes containing up to 200 volumes, which are loanable for periods of three months at a time.

The present position of the service

Staff. The Board now employs a staff of 22, including the following officers:

Chief Librarian	1	Library Clerks	2
Senior Librarian	1	Clerical Staff	3

Accountant	1	Clerk Typist	1
Personal Secretary	1	Copy Typist	2
Trainee Librarians	1	Driver	1
Senior Library Assistant	3	Messenger	2
Library Assistant	1	Watchmen	2
			22

The three trainee librarians are currently attending various library schools. Only the Chief and Senior Librarians are fully trained librarians. The Senior Library Assistant and the Library Assistant are only partially trained. The present size of staff is therefore inadequate, even for the headquarters only. But it is hoped that from the beginning of the coming financial year in July, there will be enough funds to enable the Board to engage a cataloguer and two junior librarians for the headquarters. It is also hoped that the basic staff for the first area library, which is due to be started at Kisumu on the shores of Lake Victoria, will also be recruited at the same time.

Staff and training problems. One of the serious problems which the Board has had to face and which it still has to face is that of obtaining suitably qualified staff with a fair amount of experience. In the first place, there are not enough local people who fulfil these requirements. In the second place, where expatriates can be obtained, the financial implications are often fairly prohibitive for two reasons:

(*a*) Expatriates with experience have to be given considerable inducements to leave their jobs in the home countries to come to Kenya.

(*b*) It usually costs more to induce such persons to come to Kenya than it does to pay local persons.

When these factors are coupled with the fact that funds are usually in short supply on the local scene, library development does tend to stagnate until suitably qualified local persons can be found and this cannot be easily timed either, as it also depends on whether funds are available to recruit trainees before they are sent to library schools.

It is considered here that the shortage cannot be arrested

until a steady supply of local librarians has been achieved and hence the answer is in the establishment of a good local library school, supplemented by scholarships to other library schools overseas. Although there is a School of Librarianship at Makerere University in Uganda, the following two bottlenecks are still to be removed:

(*a*) The East African School of Librarianship still has a considerably limited intake, due to shortage of accommodation and teaching staff. The School is therefore unable to help us to achieve our immediate aim, which is to produce at least five new librarians each year during the five-year period of planned development. It will therefore be necessary for Kenya to send two or three trainee librarians to obtain training elsewhere outside East Africa.

(*b*) The Board is in need of funds for various purposes. This need is aggravated by the fact that no specific financial provision for the training of librarians is made by the government outside the Board's budget. The Board is therefore placed in a position where it often has to choose between men and books. This is unsatisfactory and has also made smooth planning difficult. It is therefore being suggested that the training of librarians, like the training of other professional personnel, should be transferred to the Ministry of Education, which would then meet the necessary costs out of the normal education budget in relation to the forecasts shown in the Library Board's development plan and in consultation with the Board. This would make it possible for intending librarians to join library schools direct from high school and their training would accordingly be made cheaper, as it would then become unnecessary to pay them salaries during the period which they would spend in the library school. At the moment it is necessary for the Board not only to find funds for salaries but also to pay the necessary fees when a particular trainee enters a library school.

Alternative plan. If the Board could start and maintain a special fund outside its annual budgets for the training of librarians, then all it would ask for from the government would be the salaries of its trainee librarians. This fund would be terminated once the period of great demand for qualified librarians was passed and when the country could comfortably rely on a limited supply from library schools. It is therefore appropriate to make an appeal here to fellow librarians overseas who are in a position to assist, to think seriously about our needs for qualified librarians and to respond to our appeal as a matter of urgency.

Accommodation. The present headquarters are housed in four separate wood and iron blocks, which are situated slightly away from the city centre. These blocks do not offer adequate space, they are fairly old and, especially because they are wooden-walled, they constitute a rather serious fire risk. However, the government is aware of these facts and it is hoped that in due course funds will be made available for the construction of a proper headquarters building, which it is estimated will cost about £150 000.

Book stock. It was not possible for the Kenya Government to vote money for library expansion before the Board's development plan was approved and, because the development plan was not approved until the middle of the current financial year, no specific funds have been allocated for book purchase. However, the Board inherited a stock of about 25 000 volumes from the East African Literature Bureau. To these the Board has only been able to add an equivalent number, which puts the present stock at 50 000 volumes. This stock is still very inadequate when it is considered that the estimated reading public numbers about 2 million.

It is expected that the government will be able to make a specific grant for books in its estimates for the next financial year, i.e. 1969–70, which starts in July.

The status of libraries in the national picture

While it may appear that the government is vague in its attitude towards library development, it would be false to say that the government was not interested in libraries. In passing the Kenya National Library Service Board Act, the nation has committed itself to library development. It is true that, so far, the government has been rather parsimonious in making allocations for library development, but this can be attributed to the fact that libraries are new among the public services in the country and consequently they must expect some resistance before they can gain a foothold among the old and well-known services. Besides, it must not be forgotten that funds are in short supply for all aspects of development and that the expansion and development of a given service must depend largely on the concerted effort of those whose responsibility it is to direct the services (in the case of libraries, librarians).

International cooperation

It is therefore appropriate to include a note in this paper on the importance of international cooperation among librarians, particularly in so far as this would aid library development in the developing countries. Professional associations in other fields of human endeavour have always played a big role in promoting the welfare of their profession among the rulers and financiers of their own countries, not only for the good of their own countries but also for the benefit of countries farther afield. Therefore, while librarians in Africa must first struggle to promote libraries and librarianship within their own countries, they must also appeal to their fellow librarians in other countries, which can spare the funds, know-how and the like, to enable them to bridge the gap between what they have achieved and what librarians in developing countries are trying to achieve today.

M. Wise

The Library of the University of Dar-es-Salaam[1]

University College, Dar-es-Salaam, started its first session in October 1961, with an intake of 14 students in its Law Faculty. It was the third constituent college of the University of East Africa. The Librarian arrived in December of that year, followed shortly afterwards by the two qualified Assistants, who were not augmented by any others until the middle of 1963.

The build-up of stock for immediate teaching requirements went along with forward planning for the introduction of Arts and Social Sciences, and Science several sessions later.

At this stage of Tanganyika's library development there was a well-established High Court collection, which was outstanding among the general run of small departmental government libraries in Dar-es-Salaam. The Museum had a good collection, based on the antiquarian and ethnological studies pursued there. There was a good mineralogical collection at the Geological Survey in Dodoma, and a subscription public library in Tanga was the only worthwhile representative of public-library service in the country.

Although the new College would be able to draw on resources elsewhere in East Africa, difficulties of communication made speedy use of their facilities unlikely and it was realised from the outset that self-sufficiency in major subject areas would be most necessary.

The first year was taken up with moving the growing collec-

[1] The University of Dar-es-Salaam (formerly University College, Dar-es-Salaam) was founded on 1 July 1970 and was formally inaugurated on 29 August 1970.

tion to various temporary quarters as the entire College outgrew its first premises, and with planning the new Library building as a part of the overall layout of the College site, on an area of some 800 acres on the outskirts of the city.

The site selected was chosen with a view to trying to eliminate the necessity for air-conditioning, as the expense both of installation and maintenance would have added enormously to the capital and recurrent costs. It has been found that the low hills surrounding Dar-es-Salaam are appreciably cooler than the city, and despite the situation (less than 10° south of the Equator), life is bearable for a large part of the year in the buildings that have been put up.

As with all the other buildings, careful attention was paid to the Library's alignment along the axis of the sun, to exclude direct rays, and it was built only three modules wide (90 feet) to permit maximum breeze penetration. Vertical louvres were to be hung all round the outside, as an additional barrier to the sun, and two interior courts, open to the sky, would allow additional air circulation. These courts have not been successful in this respect. The plants installed there to make interior gardens have produced more vigorous and luxuriant growth than anywhere else in the region, proving that hot-house conditions are beneficial to natural growth, even in the tropics. In addition, they are a nuisance, occupying valuable floor space in central areas, and are the cause of continual detours to get across to the other side of the sectors they intrude upon.

A considerable area around the new building was designated early on as reserved for library development and, as a part of the attempt at self-sufficiency, a technical-services unit, comprising bindery, photography unit and printing unit, was set up in a part of the ground floor. The building was planned on three floors, to give shelving for 250 000 volumes and seating for over 600 readers. Access would be restricted only to the research collection of East Africana, and reading accommodation would be provided adjacent to all sections of the stock. Wherever possible, the readers would be adjacent to the windows, and mostly at single reading tables.

There are few service points, apart from the main issue and enquiry desk, and the main workroom and administrative offices are placed adjacent, so that the problem of maintaining the service and attending to routine tasks may be most easily performed by a minimum staff during the long hours when the Library is open. Although at the time of writing the establishment is for 12 Senior Librarians, nine graduate trainees, 11 Assistants and 13 Attendants, the continuing shortage of personnel and the absences of some on full-time training schemes leaves considerably less than the total of these numbers to operate a week of 91 opening hours, spread over all seven days.

By 1969 the student population had increased to more than 1 400. This is not spectacular by comparison with the first eight years of many universities, but in this country, where standards are being set for the first time, the Library is constantly struggling to meet the demands made upon it.

University College received its finance from the home government, and has had considerable capital sums and gifts of equipment, including books, from any countries. While these various grants and gifts have been invaluable in developing the campus at a great rate, there have been drawbacks to some of the conditions imposed by donors. The Library's American lighting system will have to be overhauled at considerable expense to avoid the necessity of continuing to import replacements from the United States, as the manufacturing standards differ from those of Britain and other countries whose electrical goods are normally available from local dealers.

The Library's stock has been built up according to immediate teaching requirements, allied to long-term forward planning, as far as it could be applied. The situation common to librarians of receiving requests for material that is not in stock yet is required for use within a few days is aggravated in Dar-es-Salaam by the distance from suppliers. The bookshops of East Africa are not able to carry the wide range of books that may be demanded by university readers, and the manager of the College Bookshop is hampered by the same problems that the Librarian has. A sea-mail delivery of between three and four months separates Dar-es-Salaam from its dealers in Europe and the United States, so that considerable forward planning of the book stock is essential. It has been found that this problem does not decrease with the Library's growth, as it is often assumed that such a large collection is almost certain to contain what may be wanted for teaching purposes.

A detailed system of library purchase, based on the selections of an interested member of each teaching department, was established in the early days to coordinate purchases and to assist in planning for future needs. This worked satisfactorily in the early days, but with the growth of departments and the departure of many founder members of the staff, it has proved difficult to maintain, to the detriment of the system that had been set up. At the time of writing the lack of subject specialists on the Library's staff who should have time to devote to book selection makes itself felt.

Exchange relationships have brought considerable enrichment to the whole collection. The Library's situation, at the university of a developing country, was, to be honest, traded upon during the early years, and many wealthy institutions gave freely material of considerable value for almost no return. The development of this College's research and publication programmes has produced a growing volume of material that can now be sent on exchange, and our first benefactors are getting some useful return for their generosity. The Library now sends out many government and research documents, in addition to its own bulletin and occasional publications. It can also offer copies of material microfilmed on the spot from the country's manuscript records and newspapers.

The Research Collection has been built up as one devoted generally to East Africa, with a natural emphasis on Tanzania. The government-documents section benefited greatly from the amount of material that became available during the re-arrangement of government departments shortly after Independence. The purchase of private collections, the incorporation of the National Museum collection as a branch library, and the acquisition of microfilm and printed material, especially from British and German sources, have enriched the historical background of the collection. The enactment of the Legal Deposit Act in 1963, with this Library as a beneficiary, has ensured an automatic flow of most current publications in Tanzania.

In addition to the important collection of government documents that forms a part of the Research Collection, the regular receipt of current official publications from many countries, especially other African states, provides a valuable basis for African studies in general. The Library is also a depository for publications of the United Nations and its subsidiary organizations, and a considerable amount of material has been acquired that predates the establishment of the depository in 1963. These have been found to be in use at a rate that astonished the Library staff, until it was appreciated how important official documents are in studying all aspects of the economy of underdeveloped countries.

The Library of Congress Classification was adopted and separate author and alphabetical subject catalogues were created, according to the Library of Congress practice. It was decided to use the system with few reservations or amendments, so as to benefit to the greatest possible extent from the provision of its ready-made cataloguing service. Bearing in mind the shortage of cataloguers and the fact that for many years they would be drawn from a number of different countries, it was felt that the international, even though Americanised, basis of the Congress system would be most readily understood by people from such varying backgrounds. Its printed catalogue and periodical lists of additions and revisions to the classification schedules and subject headings have imposed a uniformity of practice which has persisted through many changes of staff.

The Library has amended the schedules only in respect of the outdated tables that refer to eastern Africa. The subject headings have been accepted and amplified occasionally by inserting references from English usage to the American expressions that are sometimes at variance with the terminology that prevails in East Africa. Both author and subject catalogues contain history cards that guide the user through the changes of name that are imposed upon government departments and even countries. The introduction of Swahili headings, following the declaration of Swahili as the national language of Tanzania in 1967, has been made easy by adding this information to the entries on the history cards.

Because there was no reliable commercial binder in the

country who could undertake work on the scale required, the Library set up its own bindery and has trained the staff necessary to maintain it. Unfortunately, in view of the demands made on it, the output still lags far behind what is desirable, as so many non-College requests for its services are received in what is still basically a domestic concern for manual binding. A similar situation prevails in the printing unit, whose simple presses in cramped quarters are regarded by prospective customers as capable of producing full-scale bookwork. The photographic unit is best able to cope with requests for work, as its microfilming equipment has been increased sufficiently to cope with the demand for the time being, and a good electrostatic copying machine has been installed as a substitute for the Xerox copier, which cannot be serviced in this country.

The staff structure is based on graduate and professionally qualified Assistant Librarians. The competition throughout the country's economy for the graduate makes it extremely difficult to attract the required number of trainee Assistant Librarians. The government's system of controls over the movement of graduate manpower does not accord enough importance to the requirements of librarianship at present, and the annual intake is continually below what is needed to sustain this Library's progress, employing local personnel. The introduction of compulsory National Service two years ago, although of great overall benefit to the people who serve and to the national ethos, does in fact set back the post-graduate training of librarians. However, the re-arrangement of the period in camp so as to occupy the months between leaving school and entering university will soon eliminate the present time waste.

The competition in the labour market also makes itself felt in the recruitment of School Certificate holders for training for a minimum of one year before attending the course for the Certificate in Librarianship at Makerere University. On their return they are better equipped to meet the demands of their supporting roles under the Assistant Librarians in each section. The routine tasks of shelving, book preparation, filing catalogue entries, and checking readers at the entry control point are performed, usually under supervision, by the

Library Attendants. These are personnel who have not passed the School Certificate examination and whose prospects in the Library at present leave some room for improvement. It is hoped to gain acceptance for a promotion scheme based on a form of trade test. This would be similar to those that have been devised for artisans in the mechanic trades, but it will be appreciated that it is more difficult to set a test that will show how good a young man has become at simple, although very important tasks in a library. But it is only by gaining acceptance for a system of promotion that the more interested Attendants can be kept.

Cooperation between the Librarians of the three Universities in East Africa is maintained by regular meetings. The free interchange of plans for developing services has led to mutual benefit in several instances. It was in no small measure due to their participation in discussions on library education, and the willingness of Makerere University College to accept its librarian's recommendations that the School of Librarianship was established in 1963. The exchange of catalogue entries for local material has been assisted by the compilation of union catalogues of East Africana within the former University of East Africa. A system of priorities in offering duplicates has given the greatest opportunity to each library to build up its stock from resources already within the region. Regrettably, exchange of senior staff has not yet taken place, due to continuing shortage of personnel and pressure of work at each institution.

This Library has maintained a bibliography of East African material on punched cards, regardless of whether the items are held. Every effort is made to obtain the items recorded, and the entries state the source of the entry for the items that have not been obtained for the Library's collection. The data punched is designed to give a simple series of references to broad subject coverage, by decade of publication, country or countries studied, and form of publication. The entry is on a 5″ by 3″ catalogue card and it is not possible to provide for very detailed data-punching in such a small area. It is hoped that the bibliography will, increasingly, be of use to bibliographers, as the simple method of scanning permits retrieval on a broad subject basis, and the entries are carefully compiled to a standard suitable for photographic reproduction or for typesetting without the need for further editing. In addition, the bibliography is an extra to the working catalogues and could be taken apart without impairing the work of the research collection.

The Library Bulletin and Accessions List contains reproductions of catalogue entries for new accessions. It also publishes occasional lists of all material received on legal deposit. It is supplying the substance of a national bibliography, and its catalogue entries for local publications can be used by the Library of Congress in its Accessions List of the publications of eastern Africa. No other form of national bibliography exists yet and, as this Library receives all Tanzanian publications on legal deposit, its systematic listings are the basis for it. The project of compiling an indexed national bibliography is the subject of frequent discussion but awaits the availability of the personnel to undertake and maintain the work that it would involve.

The National Archives Office has not developed physically on a permanent site since Independence in the same way as the University Library. In an attempt to reduce to a minimum the publication of or even competition for holdings of materials of common interest and the technical services to perform similar functions, such as binding, repair of documents and photography, steps were taken to get agreement to build a headquarters for the Archives Office on the University site, adjacent to the Library. At the time of writing, agreement in principal exists, but the finance is not forthcoming to put up a building. The Archives Office continues to operate from several impermanent and unsuitable buildings around the capital. It has been allocated for the future a building adjacent to the University Library and its eventual construction will go far towards establishing an unrivalled research centre for all aspects of Tanzanian history, with an adequate technical-services unit for repair work and reproduction.

The University of East Africa was divided into its components in 1970. Each became the national university of its country but maintains cooperative activities on a basis that will be set out in the forthcoming report on higher education in East Africa. For several years planning has gone ahead to set up faculties for essential studies that need to be duplicated to serve the requirements of each country. The University of Dar-es-Salaam has had a Faculty of Medicine in the city for about 2 years, and started a Faculty of Agriculture at Morogoro, 125 miles away, in 1969. Each of these has to be provided with a library and the services have been established, once more in spite of staff shortages. The new Medical Library is being built on the Faculty site, which was formerly a medical-training centre, and was completed early in 1970. The new Agriculture Library is being planned to replace the inadequate building at present in use on the site of the former Agricultural Training College.

At present it is more convenient to service the Agriculture Faculty from the main Library, and the centralization of ordering and cataloguing gives a surer foundation to the collection than could be achieved by the present staff of the Faculty library. A lesser degree of centralization is practised in regard to the Medical Library, whose librarian can more easily call upon the main Library for assistance, while retaining a greater participation in the ordering and cataloguing of medical material.

The main Library was extended in 1969-70, chiefly to accommodate more readers, but also to give more space to the periodicals collection and workroom areas. Another current building project will rehouse the Technical Services Unit in more adequate premises, sited so as to be equidistant from the Library and the projected National Archives Office. Thus, the Library complex will have begun to take shape. Situated close to the centre of the expanding University, with adequate land reserved for all its projects, will be a main Library, housing over 300 000 volumes and 600 readers. Adjacent is the site for the National Archives Office. Between the two will be the joint technical services, and a more distant project envisages a separate research library, which would release the whole of the original Library building for use as a collection of undergraduate reading.

T. Nilsson

The Library and Adult Education in Tanzania: A Discussion

Is political education a fundamental part of the infrastructure? Can popular movements develop even when people are illiterate? Cannot adult education be given unless people are literate? Are books essential? These were some of the questions which came up in a round-table discussion on "Adult Education and Library Work in Tanzania", held in Dar-es-Salaam in July 1969.

The discussion was initiated by a request from the Scandinavian Institute of African Studies that I should write a paper about adult education in Tanzania to be published in this book. In view of my limited knowledge of the subject and the importance of getting Tanzanian views on Tanzanian matters, this round-table discussion was arranged as a complement to other individual contributions to this book.

When this discussion took place, the participants were aware of the Tanzanian Government's intention to introduce widespread changes in the field of adult education. These changes, which are still being worked out in detail, are outlined in the first part of this paper and in the Appendix. The second part of the paper briefly explains the library services at present available to the adult educationist and student in Tanzania, while the third and final part presents an edited version of the discussion.

Revolutionary changes in adult education in Tanzania

In the first paragraph on adult education in the Second Five-year Plan,[1] it is said that the main emphasis of adult education in the 1969–70 period will be on rural development. It will include agricultural techniques and crafts, health education, house crafts, simple economics and accounting, and education in politics and the responsibilities of the citizens.

It will be the duty of the Ministry of National Education and a newly appointed department for adult education to carry out this part of the Second Plan. One of the great tasks is to turn all the primary schools in the country into "community schools", not only serving the children but also meeting educational demands from the adults in the villages. Adult-education officers will be responsible to the Ministry for the co-ordination and development of new resources and activities on regional, district and local levels.

On the one hand, adult education will be a new part of the duties of the already available schools, which previously only taught their ordinary students. This does not mean, on the other hand, that the more than 40 agencies, ministries or national organisations which have been dealing with adult education up to now will be unemployed or released from their adult-education responsibilities. Instead, a National Co-ordination Committee will make the best use of all available resources, including the great number of experienced organisers and teachers and all sorts of educational facilities that exist throughout the country. Co-ordinating bodies will be set up at regional and district levels as well. As in other fields of development, priorities and the contents of adult-education programmes have to be in line with national plans and needs.

It is obvious that this spirit will make an impact and bring changes in some of those adult-education institutions in Tanzania which up to now have offered their adult-education programmes more or less independently.

The Institute of Adult Education at the University of Dar-

---

[1] The full text is given as an appendix to this paper.

es-Salaam is already involved in this new spirit and change. Instead of providing courses for already well-educated people (as an extension body of the University), it will increasingly be concerned in the government's plan for mass education. Since the beginning of the Second Plan period (1 July 1969) the Ministry of National Education and the Tanganyika African National Union (TANU) have asked that the Institute's resources should be devoted to the training of those several hundreds and thousands of adult educators and administrators who will be involved in the new and nation-wide adult-education machinery. One category to be trained is primary-school teachers, who will be dealing with adult education in addition to their work with children. Before the Second Five-year Plan, none of Tanzania's primary-school teachers received any adult-education training during their studies at teacher-training colleges. In the new plan, these training centres are called Colleges of National Education (CNE) and all new primary-school teachers will have adult-education training as a part of their curriculum. All the 17 CNEs in Tanzania now have their own specialist teachers in adult education, who are teaching the new primary-school teachers how to deal with adults. The first courses for training these specialists from the CNEs were held during late 1969 and were conducted by the Institute of Adult Education at the request of the Ministry of National Education.

The Institute is also involved in the training of 60 district education officers recently appointed by the Ministry. This training programme, which lasts for three months at Kivukoni College, consists of subjects such as adult-education methods and techniques, study-circle technique, political education, planning and administration, production of study material and study guides, etc.

The training of different categories of teachers and administrators will continue for a long time and is of far more importance than providing courses in French or advanced English for a small group of already well-educated people. In both cases resources and man-power are needed. It is obvious that the mass-education programme for social and economic development required by the government and the TANU must receive all the support it needs, before any amount of manpower or money can be spent on other more "luxury" programmes. This change in the role of the Institute of Adult Education has not yet resulted in any changes in its constitution. But I believe that these will soon come.

I also believe that most organisations and institutions providing adult education today will find not less but much more purpose in their work when they are playing their part in a coordinated programme under the Ministry.

We are still waiting for further details about the division of responsibilities among all the adult-education bodies working in Tanzania, but for the present discussion it may be of use to recognise that a revolutionary development of adult education is on the way in the Second Five-year Plan.

Every adult-education body is expected to organize adult-education activities around aspects of development to which it is able to contribute. The Ministry of Health is expected to give health education, the Ministry of Agriculture to help in agriculture, etc. The Institute of Adult Education is to train staff, prepare books, carry out research and run the Correspondence Institute. The Ministry of National Education is to interpret policy, co-ordinate activities and act as the main administrator of the policy.

The Library and adult education

When the discussion on "Books and Adult Education" was first planned, it was hoped that it would result in a basic reassessment of the place of books in an adult-education programme devised by a developing country. To this end, the following questions were circulated to the participants in advance of the discussion:

Are books essential, desirable or completely irrelevant in the context of an adult-education class or study group? The answers may well be different for different types of groups in different settings.

If books have a part to play, what kind of books? Who

should supply them—the students, the tutor or the library service?

What kind of book supply is required? How should it be organised?

To what extent and in what way should libraries be linked to the adult-education movement?

In the event, this fundamental re-assessment did not materialise—in fact one of the more striking features to emerge was the underlying assumption made by most of the participants that books are an essential and integral part of adult education. Perhaps it was foolish to expect otherwise. Any attempts which are made to relegate the book to a minor role in man's affairs or to discuss its diminished stature in a world increasingly dominated by television and other forms of mass media tend to have an unreal air. For the moment, and indeed for the foreseeable future, the book is indeed an indispensable tool and though education can obviously be undertaken without it, the effectiveness and durability of such education is likely to be suspect.

If it is accepted that books are essential to adult education or, at least, have an important part to play, just how do students in Tanzania gain access to books? The discussion touches on this point, but does not really answer it, and a few brief factual notes may therefore not be out of place in a publication concerned with library work and indeed may well enable the reader to appreciate more fully the interesting issues raised by the discussion.

Adult educators. The education of the future organisers and teachers of adult education and the conduct of research programmes in the field of adult education is a primary responsibility of the Institute of Adult Education. The provision of a library to meet the requirements of the teaching programme has been recognised. "The Institute has developed a library on adult education, distinct from its book collections for students, for the use of all adult educators. Included are books on the organisation and administration of adult education, methods and techniques for teaching adults, visual aids, research in adult education, community development, and handbooks prepared for adult education in Tanzania, as well as adult-education periodicals, catalogues and bulletins from a number of countries."

The organising and staffing of this library has presented problems. Initially professional guidance was provided by a librarian seconded from the Tanganyika Library Service. At a later stage qualified Canadian librarians were recruited through the Canadian University Service Overseas, but since the completion of their contracts, it has proved difficult to provide adequate staffing.

Adult students: Textbooks. Little or no provision is made for the supply of sets of textbooks for class use and in general students are expected to purchase their own. However, the Tanganyika Library Service provides some textbooks as part of its normal lending service and in all major branch libraries collections of the commonly used textbooks are provided for reference use. Preliminary discussions have also been held with the Library Service concerning the distribution of textbooks on loan to students enrolled in the proposed National Correspondence College.

Adult students: Background reading. Initially the Institute of Adult Education felt that it was its duty to provide general background reading for adult students enrolled in its classes and, with the assistance of a substantial grant from the USAID, libraries were established in Dar-es-Salaam, Mbeya, Moshi and Mwanza. More recently it has been accepted that students can be catered for more effectively and economically by directing them to the services offered by the Tanganyika Library Service. The services provided by the Library for students of all kinds are as follows.

In towns where branch libraries have already been established, substantial collections of books are available, both for home reading and reference, and the student can enrol as a reader without charge, as can all members of the public.

In villages services are now being established by the opening of small village libraries and the provision of mobile libraries through the rural-library-services programme. Elsewhere, responsible institutions can borrow collections of books. This loan service is free, as are all the library services, but a small refundable deposit is charged to guard against losses. This service has already been extensively used by adult-education associations and is available to listening groups organised through the Institute's "Education through Radio" programmes. The national adult-education officers are also to be provided with small collections of books for distribution to the villages in their districts.

Isolated readers are able to enrol with the National Central Library as postal readers. A small deposit is charged, but the service is otherwise provided without charge, the Library paying postage in both directions.

Literacy classes. Classes of people learning to read and write present a special problem. Until recently the solution has been to provide inexpensive primers for sale, but primers related to rural problems are now being produced and distributed in one area of Tanzania by the UNESCO Work-oriented Literacy Project. A rural-services librarian is working in close conjunction with the Project to establish village libraries to prevent lapses into illiteracy as part of the Tanganyika Library Service's rural-library programme.

Books and adult education: A discussion

The following persons participated in the discussion:

Max Broome. Director of Library Services for mainland Tanzania. Engaged in the establishment of a library service since 1963.

S. A. Klitgaard. Expert in book production. Has been working with the UNESCO Literacy Project in Tanzania for 16 months. Has had previous experience in West Africa.

A. S. Sefu. Works for the Tanganyika Library Service as Librarian of Kibaha.

P. J. Hezronie. Teacher of political education in the Political Education Department at the TANU headquarters.

J. M. Rutashobya. Responsible for rural training services in the Department of Rural Development, Ministry of Regional Administration and Rural Development. Has been in that Department for the last eight years, mainly working on the organisation and planning of rural training colleges.

M. L. M. Baregu. Rural Services Librarian, Mwanza. Concerned with the development of rural libraries for the Tanganyika Library Service.

T. Nilsson. Chairman. Resident Tutor, Institute of Adult Education. First came to Tanzania in 1967 to work on the Swedish adult-education assistance programme to Tanzania.

Nilsson

Could we, first of all, make clear, to people reading the words transcribed from the tape, what we are talking about? In Tanzania adult education is not the same topic as is discussed in Europe.

Broome

What we are talking about in Tanzania when we refer to adult education is not the type of advanced adult education that one experiences in Europe. I think we are concerned in Tanzania more with expanding adult education for the masses, for people who perhaps have no access to reading facilities and people who perhaps have had very little formal education. I think that this point has to be made clear; otherwise we may be talking at cross-purposes.

Nilsson

And what about the new developments and ideas that are now being planned for expanding adult education so that it reaches the masses?

Rutashobya

It may take a few months before we get something more concrete from the Ministry about this new set-up for adult education. I understand that the Ministry is now embarking on the training of adult-education officers, but still there is much to be worked out. A plan for leadership training has to be laid down jointly, mainly by the TANU and the Rural Development Division, especially on the spreading of the idea of *ujamaa,* the establishment of training of the adult population in the principles of *ujamaa* villages. I think that after a few months we shall be able to speak in more concrete terms about what our parts are going to be. It is right that great changes should take place. But even the Ministry itself has a lack of qualified personnel. It makes every effort to train adult educators, not only for administrative purposes, but also for introducing adult-education teaching in the teaching in the teachers' colleges. It will be one of the teachers' responsibilities to teach the mature student and to enrol people who are going to help in teaching the illiterate community. Again the Ministry of National Education is organising through the Institute of Adult Education the research programmes in adult education itself. These are things that are being worked out in a rather complete form. The Institute will also be responsible for the correspondence institute which we hope will be established in the very near future. These are the aspects we do know, but still they are not complete yet.

Nilsson

It is also said that adult education *and* political education will be provided through the same "machinery" through the same teachers and adult-education officers. Now, isn't it true that political education up to now has been a specific topic taught by political-education officers through the TANU? What are the plans for coordinating or mixing adult education in general with political education?

Hezronie

I think political education will remain as political education, but the intention is not to have a duplication of work. Whoever is, for example, a regional education officer is at the same time a political-education officer. Education in politics is an actual part of adult education. It is only taught separately when there is no programme co-ordinating all this.

So political education will be a part of a scheme that we do not yet know very much about. It would not be proper to comment on the new set-up too much at this stage. What I know is that political education will remain as political education, except that, to avoid duplication of work, the adult-education officers in charge will also be responsible for political education at district level. But what I want to add to this is that political education extends from national level to the grass-roots as part of adult education. At present we have political-education officers at regional level, but also a TANU national political-education department, which, for instance, has political-education classes for all the TANU chairmen at a series of regional courses. We have *ujamaa*-village classes, which means they are political-education classes for the implementation of the TANU policy. Now, the man in charge of adult education at district level will in the future also be responsible for political education, which does not mean that political education should not remain as a separate subject.

Baregu

May I add a point here? The way I look at political education in this country is almost the way I look at literacy work. I think that these two things are basic. Political education is a fundamental part of the infrastructure. It is preparing for education in agriculture, craftmanship, health education and everything that is basically technical or economic. In this country, with socialism and self-reliance as the basis of its policy, political education has got to move at a faster pace than the rest of adult education, so has literacy. I think these two are fundamental. And then, as Hezronie said, everything can come under political education.

Rutashobya

Can one make a distinction between political education and leadership training?

Hezronie

It depends on what kind of leadership we mean. Leadership training may be training teachers to teach, to teach or lead children perhaps. But if it is leadership, for example, for *ujamaa* villages, that is political education.

Rutashobya
Now, on that particular line, could I ask a question here? Our theme for this discussion is adult education. Adult education for what, in a Tanzanian sense? In my opinion adult education is for development purposes, following the nation's demand. We are guided by the political ideology of the party. For example, if it is about agriculture, it is agriculture based on the *ujamaa* principles. For me, I would not separate political education from the rest of adult education. It is one and the same thing. Everything that we have to teach to the adults should be based on the country's ideology.

Broome
There is a limit to the amount of pure political education that can be done. But political principles or philosophy can run through all types of adult-education classes. You may have some pure political-education classes, but if political and adult education are to be integrated in the way described by Mr. Nilsson, then fundamental principles and philosophy should run through all adult education, should underline all subjects.

Baregu
I agree with that, but there is a danger—a psychological danger. There is a thing that one can define as pure political education, purely aimed at political attitudes. It is also quite true that it crosses almost every sphere, in the attitudes that are applied to agriculture, economics and everything. But I also think there is a need to have the points of things in general, the politics, let's say, of production in this country, explained in our own ideological terms. A basic thing is that, before you can explain, let's say, agriculture, there is a need to actually lift the attitudes of the people politically, that is, to imbue them with socialist thinking. They must become good socialists, ideologically. There is a purely political way of thinking that must be put across.

Nilsson
Don't you think that this lifting up of political attitudes must be done in the same way as in literacy, where we talk about

functional literacy? Can political attitudes be lifted up, so to say, functionally? Some people may need to understand how to solve very local and practical problems before being motivated to develop an interest in national plans or ideology, or vice versa. Some people may need to understand national plans and politics before they see the link, the practical and functional link, between those plans and their own local needs.

Baregu

This is quite true. The political education in, for example, *ujamaa* villages is quite practical. They are not only taught to live together, they are doing it. I think this is the ideal, to do it very practically, when teaching political education. But for the next two or three years all the people will not live in *ujamaa* villages, and for the rest of the people, who will not be there, something theoretical has to be done. The Arusha Declaration must be explained to all. Mwalimu Nyerere's theroetical work has to be explained. These things are basic to the whole nation. A person not living in an *ujamaa* village may read and understand the pamphlet *Ujamaa Vijijini* and will thereafter make contact with a chairman of an *ujamaa* village. This is the sort of reaction I am thinking of—the explanation of basic thoughts to create spirit.

Klitgaard

A question to you, Baregu. I have got the impression that you want to keep political education and literacy in one group, because it is a question of changing attitudes. This you have repeated several times. But if I look at the Five-year Plan and look at all the subjects which you are going to teach, agriculture, health ... in my opinion all this is also a question of changing attitudes. The whole thing is a question of changing attitudes. For that reason I would agree with Mr. Rutashobya when he said "consider all these subjects together". I can't understand why you want to divide these things.

Baregu

Well, let me put it this way. During the colonial times, the Germans and the British tried to do something about health education, homecraft, simple economics—maybe not simple economics or accounting—but they carried out quite a few campaigns; some of them even got through to the man in the village. In quite a few cases those campaigns turned out to be failures. I think the question is what kind of approach you have, in leading things. What was not done was to teach people to read and write. In introducing new methods of agriculture, it is also a question of political attitude. For a long time people have only been taught how to grow, just to survive. It has to be explained that they can produce more and support the country and improve their own lives. One does not only talk about agriculture as such, not only about health, but also those basic things that one should know—such basic things as the Arusha Declaration and *Ujamaa Vijijini*. Those things that create the infrastructure for assimilating all the other progressive technical adult-education activities. I may be wrong, but I believe that these two things, political education and literacy work, have to go faster. These should be given priority now.

Rutashobya

Do you mean to tell us that there cannot be any other form of adult education unless people are literate?

Baregu

More or less. I think I can say that. More or less.

Broome

Now, let us go back to the questions on the sheet of paper Mr. Nilsson first circulated: "Are books essential?" Or "What kind of adult-education programmes can we run and what success will they have without reading materials?" Though it is true that the new pattern of adult education is not yet determined, the Ministry of National Education has already made a start on training adult educators and it is relying on teachers, as we have heard, and also on teachers who have retired—giving them "crash" courses and hoping they will make a success of it. What I think we ought to do now is perhaps to get away from the discussion on the ideology of adult education and look at the practical difficulties. We train these people. These people themselves are literate. Then they are sent out into isolated villages, where they may be the only educated people. How effective are they going to be? And how are they going to be supported? I think we should look at these questions and then also look at the type of support that perhaps we should give and the materials that they may need, to make a success of their programmes.

Nilsson

Well, are there any more comments to add to our discussion on the ideology of adult education or could we turn to these practical questions? Incidentally, I believe that the ideology or policy behind adult education does have the most practical consequences—therefore, even our discussion on ideology is to me very practical indeed. Now, don't let us turn this into a debate on semantics. I do understand and will also support Mr. Broome's suggestion. Any more comments on our previous discussion?

Rutashobya

I just want to emphasize political education as a subject in adult education. As far as the development purpose of this country is concerned, we have placed more emphasis on political education, in the first instance, because ... what follows? What follows is just schemes. I'll try to divide up adult education into two sectors. One is leadership training. Because, as far as Tanzania is concerned, the success of all adult-education programmes will depend on the leadership we get at the village level. Even in the new set-up we don't expect a primary-school teacher to take over the full organisation of adult education in the villages. First of all, all schools are not very central. Some schools are five miles from the nearest village. We don't expect adults to march five miles from the village to the school. In this case the teacher must follow the adults into the villages. We have to use the persuasion method—we are not going to force adults to school, as we do with the children. In this case we have to depend on local leaders. Now, a change of this leadership is to take first place and then we follow it with the second type of adult education, which I call schemes. All these—literacy, agriculture, health—I call them schemes. And these schemes are to be built on the village organisation. Of course, I believe in the usefulness of books in adult education and I think we now should go into the proper subject.

Nilsson

"Are books essential?" It may at first seem to be quite a silly question, but at the same time we know the fact that there are very few books and a shortage of all kinds of study material compared with the needs. Do we really need a highly developed book production and material distribution for all kinds of adult-education activities? Are there other ways, other media, to be used, besides the written word, during the time when book production and written material are under development?

Sefu

Well, apart from the written word, I think the visual film or the radio is the basic media. If we could discuss this and relate them to books and to written words in general, we may be able to develop something. The spoken word, broadcast on the radio. And also films, documentary films, especially films that explain certain things that get down to and deal with basic skills; the film on improving agriculture, for example, is a good thing. The radio has its limitations. People do not easily remember what they have heard. There is not very much organised listening. The radio system in this country is not perfect. The reception is not always accurate. All these practical problems bring me back to the written word, the book, the pamphlet, the newspaper or whatever is the basic written media we should aim at as best. Everything else I think should supplement the book or written words.

Baregu

People are likely to remember a good story told on the radio. If just presented with facts through the radio, people will find it hard to both understand and remember. In using the radio for education purposes, I think one should use stories. This brings me to the next reflection. Books are not very useful when very few people can read or are able to understand them. Perhaps the first kind of books should be the kind that encourages the leaders to learn more about their jobs and about what they are expected to do.

Rutashobya

If you take the population of Tanzania, let's say, before independence, you would find that very few people understood what *uhuru* was. There was a lot of adult education that took place between 1954 and 1961. People were attending meetings, listening to speeches, holding group discussions and so on. People became aware of the importance of becoming free. Is that not adult education?

Take another example, the missionaries. For instance, the Christians have a certain faith. Though illiterate, they become educated in that form of belief. There are a lot of things—visual aids, demonstrations, study tours, discussions, sports, dances, songs—all these are forms of adult education, depending on who organises it and the purpose behind it.

I think we could talk a lot about those forms and so on, but the topic is books, the usefulness of books in adult education. What kind of books we have, and what improvements could be made to make them useful for adult-education programmes in Tanzania. People talk about the lack of books in Swahili. The few books we have, are they suitable for our adult-education programmes? What means could we employ to improve them? These are meaningful and important questions.

Nilsson

People become aware of the importance of independence without knowing how to read and write, as Rutashobya said. A popular movement developed even when most of the people were illiterate. A lot of writers about developing countries and their problems insist that development, health and a better life depend on people's ability to read and write. That the book and literacy work are the only ways out of starvation, overpopulation, disease, low production, etc. Well, we know that knowledge can be spread by books and the written word, but are we, as human beings, entirely dependent on this media? Despite the work of UNESCO and all the national literacy programmes, the fact remains that the world produces 25 to 30 million more illiterates every single year. The literacy programmes, all depending on books and the written material for development, are doomed to failure if no other means or tools can make up the balance of needed distribution of knowledge. World development, from an educational point of view, will get worse every second, every day and every year, if human beings entirely depend on books or the written word for development.

Rutashobya

Now, what are we trying to develop when we arrange adult-education programmes? What is our aim? We are trying to develop a person as an individual in the community. Somebody who will become independent in thinking etc., someone able to find out knowledge on his own. Even if you take all the media, such as radio, visual aids, etc., it involves a lot of organisation. You need somebody to guide it and somebody who knows how to read and write. He needs a book and to be able to read instructions, perhaps with very little assistance. But I do agree with some thinkers that for development purposes, we should not wait until all people are literate before we start other forms of adult education.

If we want to improve the production aspect of the adult population now, during the Second Five-year Plan, then we cannot wait until the adults can read and write and then tell them "Well, now you can farm". What we need is a comprehensive integration of these activities. That will lead us to what Nilsson called, in the beginning, the functional approach to adult education.

Baregu

I will quote Lenin, who said: "An illiterate person is outside this field of politics. The first thing he must be taught is the alphabet." Now, I think I would be prepared to repeat that statement as I would the Lord's Prayer, if I were a Christian.

I think, fundamentally, that, even if this country had all the other media, they have their limitations. As I said before, if you can get somebody to continue reading, you can then get on to the technical business of producing material and making sure that those people on their own can read something that turns up. Many books were produced by the British in an interesting way; they were meant for people at an elementary level, but they were not read because people were not literate. And, of course, the British realised the use of producing this material. But they did not realise that this material could never get down to the person who was actually required to absorb it. In this country we cannot really get very far if we don't seriously tackle the problem of literacy on something like the Cuban scale. We must do something almost near to that. The problem is to create the rational arrangements to make this possible, in my opinion.

Nilsson

Could we for a moment discuss the problem of giving the first-stage literate person the possibility of developing the new skill? A lot of literacy programmes have been carried out, often with quite good results. People have learned the alphabet and sometimes more. But nobody likes to read or repeat the alphabet for the rest of his life. One wants to continue, to learn more and keep up interest by finding more and more information. If books, newspapers, pamphlets, etc. are not available, the person is as illiterate as before the campaign after a year or two. Let me add to the question: what is done by the organisers of literacy campaigns at the planning stage, before coming to the paradoxical situation that people have learned how to read and write but do not have anything more than their alphabet or first primer for practising their new skill?

Rutashobya

I think we will be in a better position to comment on that after, for example, we have heard something about what percentage of books in this library are available in Swahili. Then we can go on to analyse the contents of those books. Are they suitable for the rural community now, which forms 95% of our population? If that is not so, what could be done to improve the situation?

Broome

The first thing we have to accept is that a library can only work with the books that are available. This is one of the major difficulties in trying to establish any kind of library service in a developing country. The major stock of books in a library in a country like Tanzania inevitably has got to be in a language in which there is widespread publication—to begin with, anyway. Try as you may, you cannot increase the proportion of books in Kiswahili. Those books do not exist. Moreover, the books that do exist in Kiswahili are—the bulk of them—at primer level. There is very, very little to take a reader beyond very simple texts. Though we may plan and organise our libraries and though we may plan and organise the penetration of the libraries into the countryside, we shall always be working under the limitation of the lack of suitable material. We can supplement this with material which is half suitable and we do that, but we come back really to the question of book production rather than the library in the first instance. Today only 5% of the books in this library are in Kiswahili.

Nilsson

What kind of books are most needed?

Hezronie

What kind of books do you mean? Books for the masses or for the élite?

Nilsson

That's a very good question—do you have some priorities in your own mind? What is most needed? What books for the masses? What is the need of books for the so-called élite?

Broome

For the highly trained person, there is very little problem, for the scientist and so on is literate in English and there are more books published in English than in any other language in the world. Though one can argue about the suitability of some of the material for Tanzanian conditions, there is in fact a wealth of material, particularly if you talk about a discipline like science, which is universal. I think the real bottleneck comes immediately after learning the ABC. You have now got quite a large number of books produced for people who wish to learn how to read Kiswahili. You don't perhaps need very many different types at this level; those that are concerned with the mechanics of reading only. It is when a man has learned how to read and wants to exploit and expand that skill that we run into difficulties. Again perhaps we are beginning now to catch up with the demand at the very lowest level. When he tries to go beyond this stage, he is lost. There is no material or very, very little material in Kiswahili at this stage.

Rutashobya

Why should this be so? When we have an adult-education programme, knowing very well that we have several agencies, over 40 agencies, each engaged in adult education of some sort. What is the problem? The problem is to start seriously on the writing of these books. That is what each agency should do. We expected the TANU to produce some good follow-up material on political education. Not only that, but also to take part in the writing of the literacy primers, because, if we are to make our literacy programme rather functional, then the contents of these primers should be politically and culturally oriented. We don't expect somebody from outside to come and write books for us. People who are involved in these programmes should set to work seriously and write books for the adult community. Up to 1965 we had only two or three literacy primers. Then we got rid of these primers because they were not functional. Then we started again and during the last 3 years we have produced about nine primers. But this is the function of only one agency. If we could get serious about the business of writing, we could to some extent overcome this problem.

Baregu

I think that 40 agencies sounds very many. I do not believe that many of them are able to produce their own study material. Rather than to have every agency produce material, it would be better to organise all the agencies that are needed under one wing and in that way produce all the material within one large organisation. This is the way I think we can go about it.

Rutashobya

We can do it in two different ways. One is, as you have explained, by having one big organisation. That is the approach we have been following between the Ministries. A committee has been co-ordinating under the Ministry of Regional Administration and Rural Development, but the representatives were selected from Agriculture, Health, the Cooperative Education Centre in Moshi, the Ministry of Agriculture, Food and Cooperatives itself, the East African Literature Bureau and so on. It was not a full-time committee, but we have a full-time book-production officer who takes up all the follow-up work of the committee. We can expand that system and have one large national organisation for book production. That is the case in Uganda, where they have the Milton Obote Foundation, the main work of which is to produce books suitable for both Uganda and other countries. They have produced several publications that are very useful.

Another way is more the province of the Ministry of National Education. We should get the teachers' colleges, the Institute of Adult Education, etc. not only to start seriously training personnel in adult education but also writing suitable books for adults. In fact, I have been arguing this in connection with the literacy classes and so on, which according to my understanding cannot be tackled successfully. You cannot eradicate illiteracy when you have a stream of illiterate people coming in. Tanzania can now afford primary-school places for about 52% of the children. It means that 48% are following the illiteracy stream. Unless we eradicate these 48%, I do not see where we are heading, even if we apply the Cuban- or

Russian-style programmes. Unless we have full compulsory primary education, the illiteracy problem will still exist.

Hezronie

People in the villages like books which can help them to further development; which can make them go forward with the policy. What we always suggest to authors is that they can design anything in writing but they must put the main emphasis on people in rural areas. By that I mean that, if, for example, one writes a book on health education, there should always be some reference to towns, but it should mostly refer to rural places; how the rural places can get better health. I can give you an example from a previous book we had; when they talked about bilharzia, they referred to rural areas. Rural areas were identified with bilharzia. That's all. When they wanted to talk of what they called progress, they referred to towns. Whoever was in rural areas felt backward and those in urban areas felt developed. This is a conflict. Most of the people live in rural areas. That is why we say that, whatever book you write, when you want to advise people to improve their way of living, please take examples from urban villages which you are sure have improved, so that a person in Soshanya village can read about Kigamboni, which has eradicated a certain type of disease because of doing this or that. Do not give an example of a town. We suggest to authors that, when they write books, they should also quote certain aspects of *ujamaa*. The book should encourage people to live together, whatever type of book it is. If it is about music, singing together is good because it produces good tones, and they like melody and harmony; whatever it is, it should emphasise the *ujamaa* theory. What was said in the Arusha Declaration can also be said practically in every other field. What I am trying to say is that all their examples should drive them to the villages and also, whatever examples are given, they should refer to the principles of *ujamaa*.

Nilsson

Does the TANU recommend *ujamaa* villages to set up libraries and do you cooperate with the Library Service in this?

Hezronie

Indeed we do. We advise the *ujamaa* villages to set up libraries but not in 1969; we thought it should come after the villages were settled.

Baregu

May I add a point here? So far, we have made great progress in cooperating with the Department of *Ujamaa* Villages at the TANU headquarters. We produced a questionnaire in order to find the rate of literacy in established villages, and asked people if they had any books in their own houses and if they were ready to establish some kind of literacy changes. So far, in our rural library project *ujamaa* villages stand out as major places which must be served.

Klitgaard

Mr. Baregu, we have a good tradition that we should always argue. I refer to our earlier discussions and will return to the question of distribution again. If I could get you in a corner, I think I should get you to agree.

Baregu

I am basically in agreement. All I am saying is that I go back to my village when I am on leave and I know fairly well what place a book has. I know that somebody reads to my mother. She asks my young brother or even me to read aloud to her. I think my mother would be shocked if I said: "Mother, why don't you go out and buy that book?" Well, because I am connected with the library, she may say, "Yes", but another mother would not.

Klitgaard

I am glad you said that. But there is an important question: How do we motivate people? How do we motivate other mothers to go to the shop and buy books? The question of motivation seems to me to be the most important one also in adult education. One day, in a further discussion, I think that should be the main topic.

Baregu

One way in which I think we could operate is to establish library services at the cooperative primary-society level. A few books are supplied by the society and then people can be asked to contribute more books. In Musoma we are trying this and they are trying to get people to contribute as a community. That is in line with the socialist outlook. If people learn to buy books for this contribution, there is also a chance that people will learn to buy books for themselves. I think this is one way of doing it.

Klitgaard

I have twenty suggestions for distribution. We have no time to discuss all of them. But now I have got the twenty-first. If you get people into the habit of contributing books, you also teach them to buy books for themselves. That's fine.

Broome

What I am interested in knowing is how much motivation already exists anyway. It is a common experience in a library that the people using it find books in the library and ask if they can buy them. That is a reflection of the poor commercial book outlets in this country. When we started first, we had a tremendous problem with people taking books and coming in the following day saying they had lost them. And really, they were using the library as a bookshop.

Now, Sefu, you have gone out with your rural service around Kibaha. To what extent have you found amongst the rural people around Kibaha any desire to buy books from you?

Sefu

Not in Kibaha itself. That is because they know that we are not selling books. But in the surrounding countryside it happens very often that people want to buy books.

Broome

So the motivation does exist. I would suggest that the motivation is, in fact, inspired by the establishment of the library. These people are often exposed to books for the first time.

The library itself, by providing its services, is creating motivation.

Klitgaard

Yes, library and book distribution go hand in hand.

Baregu

We are providing a service and we can lose books. But people get used to books and I think booksellers in a sense get an advantage from those losses. When books are spread, you can come and sell.

Klitgaard

I agree that the library should come in first, but then I hope that you agree that it is high time that we started thinking of the distribution system in this country. We have been thinking of libraries during the last few years and now it is time to think of distribution.

Baregu

Yes, but you must agree that the library is a kind of distributor.

Klitgaard

Yes, but it is not enough. You must also develop the need of having one's own books. People must learn to think: "This is a book I want to have. It should be my property."

Baregu

Well, but that is not a very socialistic way of thinking. Ownership is not so much of a problem.

Nilsson

Are not people also interested in getting more than knowledge from books? Not only skill or practical instructions for work that may interest them. People may also obtain pleasure from reading a book, whoever is the owner. The intellectual enjoyment should be a part of the motivation.

We now have talked about the shortages of teachers and books, the importance of adult education, the lack of distribution of reading material, etc. Why not try to combine those needs and use some rational ways to overcome the difficulties? For instance, why not have books on recorded tape and let people listen to it, illiterate as well as literate? Maybe the most motivated group contains those people who have just learnt how to read and write but for whom there is not enough reading material available for continuous reading. Why not distribute the contents of books by loudspeaker in the villages, in community centres, under the mango trees, etc.?

If well arranged and edited, you will get a lot of people to listen and enjoy it. That may be the best way to motivate people both to continue the practice of reading and also to write and to buy books.

Baregu

If I understand Nilsson right, he suggests loudspeakers and recorded books to be distributed orally to people. I think it is a very good idea.

Broome

This method has its limitations. It takes a long time to read a book. But what should happen is similar to what we are trying to do in our children's libraries. We don't actually read the book to the children, but we give an indication of the contents of the book in telling a story, and this motivates the child to read the book. This sort of thing is very valuable to make people want to read.

Klitgaard

The risk with your system, Nilsson, is that you may succeed so well with that system that people will not think it worth while to read.

Nilsson

I would like to refer to the question again: "Are books essential?" Do we really have to depend on books entirely? Couldn't a lot of information needed for development work be distributed by using technical equipment and modern teaching aids, at least as alternatives to the mass distribution of the book itself? We did not come to this stage in our earlier discussion, but now I tend to believe that you do agree that the *contents* of books, the most essential information of importance to the people, can be distributed by other methods than by mass distribution of reading materials.

Baregu

This is absolutely acceptable and a good idea to try. I don't know if Radio Tanzania has any book-reading programmes?

Broome

They used to run a BBC series.

Hezronie

The TANU and Radio Tanzania have organised a series on political education. But they are reading word by word in a not too stimulating manner. We are discussing how to improve this programme.

Nilsson

One way for improvement may be to combine such listening with study-circle activities, discussions, exhibitions, demonstrations of tools and methods, etc. The combination of the spoken word with practical exercise is most useful in adult education. The distance between theory and reality must be as short as possible.

Broome

We have already thought of reading circles out in the villages. One literate person reads to a group of people. The use of tape recordings is also very useful. These methods could work together.

Nilsson

Trying to speculate a bit for the future, I do believe that it might soon be realistic to plan for very radical improvements in mass-education efficiency by using such things as mobile (circuit) TV units projecting on to screens of drive-in format in villages. Local leaders and teachers can talk and demonstrate to the people through those mobile studios, using both video tapes and films. Another thing we should foresee and plan for is educational programmes, both radio and TV, launched by international bodies and broadcast by satellites to all the countries who want it. Such programmes can even be edited and recorded locally, if necessary.

To put an end to this discussion, I just want to thank you on behalf of the Scandinavian Institute of African Studies. Thank you for your contributions.

A comment on the discussion

The following remarks on the discussion were made by Mr. Paul Mhaiki, of the Ministry of National Education in Dar-es-Salaam:

"The discussion is good and covers most aspects of libraries in developing countries. Most interesting is the suggestion of the latest methods, such as taped books for use in study circles, video tapes and films. Perhaps some time will pass before developing countries can afford to use these facilities on a large scale. The point which should be discussed, I feel, is the problem of producing books for rural libraries. Books in Swahili are very limited in number; there is a great need for the writing of books in Swahili for adults in rural areas. The Adult Education Section of the Ministry of National Education makes arrangements to organize workshops for writing books in Swahili on topics of national interest."

Appendix

Adult Education in Tanzania's Second Five-year Plan for Economic and Social Development
(1 July 1969–30 June 1974)

The main emphasis in adult education in this Plan period will be on rural development. It will include simple training in agricultural techniques and craftsmanship, health education, housecraft, simple economics and accounting, and education in politics and the responsibilities of the citizen. In rural areas, virtually the whole of this work will be conducted in Swahili. Literacy will be included in response to popular demand, as people become aware of its functional importance.

The needs of urban areas may be assumed in part to be met by existing organizations, notable by the University Institute of Adult Education, but there is room for the expansion of simple vocational classes, for which provision is not made by existing training institutions.

The characteristic feature of adult education is that various organizations participate. Among them are government departments, the TANU, the UWT, the co-operative movement and the Churches. Part of the work to be done is the co-ordination and encouragement of existing activities and another part is the promotion of new activities.

The main limiting factor is the scarcity of experienced staff. Further, it will be impossible to devote capital funds to the building of new centres for adult education during the Plan period and consequently full use must be made of existing premises. Fortunately, this necessity is unlikely to impede development.

Development proposals

The general principle is to place the main organising responsibility on the primary school. The school will then become a community educational centre, at which the provision of primary education is only one function. A school so conceived will increasingly become a focal point for the total educational needs of the community, rather than serving as a somewhat detached institution for the education of children.

The general responsibility for the adult-education activities of the centre will rest with the headmaster.

It will be the duty of the headmaster to ascertain community needs to identify suitable instructors and to arrange classes. Each headmaster will have at his disposal a small grant for equipment and materials.

Instruction will be given by persons supplied by Ministries and organizations or by individuals in the neighbourhood who are competent to give instruction. The development of this programme will be phased over a number of years, building on experience as it is gained. Administrative, capital and recurrent costs will be minimized by making maximum use of the existing structure. The Institute of Adult Education will assist the programme by providing training for the cadre of education officers, who will provide leadership for its development.

The Institute of Adult Education

A word must be added about the special role of the Institute of Adult Education. Reference has already been made to the Institute's function in urban areas and to the training of adult-education officers. As a body responsible for research, the Institute will also be well placed to follow up the developing programme outlined above and to assess its usefulness. But in addition to these important tasks, it is envisaged that the Institute will carry out a pilot project aimed at the establishment of a National Correspondence College, to serve literate but isolated persons throughout the country who wish to enlarge their knowledge and understanding, particularly in subjects of importance to national development.

N. O. Arunsi

The Library and Adult Education in Tanzania: A Survey

Adult education is a complex subject to define. The problem of definition arises from the complexity of the adult population throughout the world and the variety of educational activities for adults. Whereas the largest untapped source of manpower for skilled and high-level occupations in Africa is the adult population, the contrary is true in the more advanced and developed countries of Europe and America. Therefore, with a high percentage of illiteracy in nearly all the African countries, it would be insufficient to define adult education merely as "a process of continuing education". It is understandable for an adult in the developed countries with the advantage of some kind of formal education or technical training to regard adult education as a process of continuing education and life-long self-improvement. To the illiterate adult in Africa with no formal education or training in the "modern" sense, adult education is synonymous with illiteracy eradication. He or she needs adult literacy education first of all to become literate. This newly acquired literacy is not an end in itself but only a step in a programme of continuing education. Here lies the crux of the matter and, in my opinion, it is important for any definition to recognize this major distinction.

The second part of the problem of definition is the variety of educational activities for adults, which are more often sponsored by non-educational than formal educational institutions. For instance, many non-educational organizations and institutions carry out adult-education programmes to assist in achieving their goals. Hence, ministries, social movements, governmental agencies, cultural societies, churches, voluntary associations, co-operatives and industries organize educational and training activities for adults. The majority of the teaching staff are often part-time teachers of adults engaged in other occupations.

The concept of adult education in Africa therefore should be much wider than "continuing education". Any general definition of the term has to include such activities as literacy education, university extension, correspondence courses, extension services, residential colleges, technical colleges and mass education. These activities are treated in more detail in the next section of this paper. It is the detailed account of the organisation and development of the various activities which form the history of adult education in Africa. This history dates back to the recent past. While the history of adult education in Australia dates back to the 1890's, the 1850's in the Scandinavian countries and even earlier in England and America, it may not be wholly correct to say that the late 1940's marked the beginning of adult education in Africa. Such a statement would merely reflect a somewhat restricted view of adult education in the historical sense. Actually, adult education in Africa and in Tanzania in particular goes back to many years, even centuries, for adult education played an important part in traditional education in Africa. For example, in the chapter on "System of Education" in *Facing Mount Kenya,* Jomo Kenyatta states: "In the following description, it will be found that education begins at the time of birth and ends with death. The child has to pass various stages of age-grouping with a system of education defined for every status in life." He then describes the traditional types of adult education among the Kikuyu, continuing through adulthood, even among the elders.

The urgent need for mass education gave rise to a number of regional conferences (1956–65)[2] between the developing countries of Africa, Asia and Latin America and the UNESCO,

[2] UNESCO: *Educational Planning: A World Survey of Problems and Prospects.* Paris 1970, pp. 29 ff.

to work out plans for the development of education and also to determine the shortest and most economic means of achieving the desired goals.

The Addis Ababa and Tananarive Conferences of 1962 and the Abidjan Conference of African Ministers of Education (March 1964) worked out the objectives of all the three educational levels, primary, secondary and higher, covering a 20-year period between 1960 and 1980.

In 1957 the UNESCO launched a major project for the extension of primary education in Latin America. The project produced good results and demonstrated the value of the regional approach to many problems involved in expanding educational facilities. This inspired further surveys of the educational needs of Asia, the Arab states, the Middle East and Africa. One of the most significant facts which was revealed by these surveys was the high illiteracy rate of about 80–85 per cent, which at that time was nearly twice the average world figure.[3]

(i) The high rate of illiteracy and the still incomplete development of the educational system.

(ii) The number of pupils failing to complete their schooling, primary and secondary, and therefore receiving an insufficient preparation for their working life.

(iii) The number of young people who return from their primary schooling to largely illiterate communities, where they are deprived of the opportunity of expanding or even of maintaining the knowledge they have acquired.

(iv) The rapidity of economic and social change, which means that education received today is already inadequate for tomorrow.

In March 1964 the UNESCO organized a Conference at Abidjan in the Ivory Coast with "The Planning and Organisation of Literacy and Adult-education Programmes in Africa" as the theme. One of the problems discussed during this conference was the drop-out of students in literacy classes. The Conference agreed that this drop-out was more generally due

---

[3] Ringmar, Torgil: Adult Education in Africa: Possibilities and Problems, in *Library Work in Africa,* Scandinavian Institute of African Studies, Uppsala 1966, pp. 46 ff.

to unsuitable teaching materials and inefficient teachers than to lack of keenness among the adults. In other words, adults are to some extent keen to learn but, owing to lack of teaching materials and unskilled, untrained teachers, many of them drop out. It was also revealed from the reports given by some of the delegates that the best results had been obtained where the actual teaching of reading and writing had been preceded, accompanied and followed by general education in matters of interest to the adult students by the spoken word. In other words, adult students need motivation.

The second problem discussed by the Conference was functional literacy. An adult should not only acquire the ability to read and write but should be equipped with an intellectual training that will be useful in technical work. The Conference finally supported the implementation of the "World Experimental Literacy Programme". The strategy of this programme was to stimulate literacy in relation to its contribution to economic and social development. This policy is the basic concept of the UNESCO programme using the "selective approach method", in which efforts are concentrated in a small number of areas or regions.

The policy is to help countries identify the areas and sectors of the working population, where the contribution of literacy is most productive, aiming progressively to cover the whole population. An area of industrial development with a high population of illiterate workers, for instance, might include centres for "on-the-job literacy teaching", leading directly to vocational and technical training. In such an area the eradication of illiteracy in the existing labour force, the provision of literacy education in the neighbourhood of industrial centres for rural youth, who seek employment in urban areas and the provision of elementary technical or vocational training will increase productivity and thus reduce costs, making better use of capital invested.[4]

The Republic of Tanzania decided to adopt this policy after the 1966 UNESCO mission carried out by an educationist

[4] UNESCO: Functional Literacy as a Factor in Development. International Education Year 1970. IEY Special Unit No. 1, UNESCO, Paris 1970.

and an economist. The details of this planning system in Tanzania, a new approach in fighting illiteracy, are discussed in the following section.

Adult education in Tanzania

The year 1970 was "Adult Education Year" for Tanzania.[5] His Excellency the President of the United Republic of Tanzania made this proclamation in his New Year radio message to the nation. Quoting one of the vows of the Tanganyika African National Union (TANU), "I shall educate myself to the best of my ability and use my education for the benefit of all", he announced that high priority would be given to the work of educating adults, in order to achieve the fulfilment of this vow.

Plans by the government and by the TANU, said His Excellency, are not enough by themselves and he emphasized the necessity for all of us to work together if 1970 is really to be "Adult Education Year". This Presidential proclamation is bound to raise the pertinent question, Why adult education in 1970? In order to answer this question and to put the post-independence educational problems into their proper context, some understanding of the historical development of education in Tanzania is necessary.

History of education in Tanzania

The history of formal education in Tanzania has been relatively short. It dates back to the end of the 19th century and was, until recently, dominated by the missionaries. Catholic and Protestant schools were opened in various parts of the country. The colonial government's education policy was one

---

[5] "1970 is Adult Education Year". New Year broadcast by President Nyerere, published in (*a*) *The Standard of Tanzania*, 1 January 1970, p. 1, and (*b*) *The Nationalist of Tanzania*, 1 January 1970, p. 1.

of segregation. Schools were uni-racial and each racial group raised a levy from its own members for education. Administratively, there was a European Department, an Indian Education Department and a Goan Education Department (non-Africans). The colonial government was content to leave the education of Africans in the hands of the missionary bodies and did no more than set up an Advisory Council on African Education in 1925.[6] In its Annual Report of 1937 the Education Department stated that, besides one secondary school for 24 Africans in Tabora, where the sons of chiefs underwent a six-year course of training in native government, there were 300 for Africans (29 942 pupils), 52 for Indians (3 863 pupils) and 18 for Europeans (823 pupils).[7] About one-third of the schools for Africans were managed by the government, leaving the rest almost entirely under the auspices of missions which were only supervised by the government. In 1947 a Ten-year Plan was drawn up and in the 1952 Annual Report of the Education Department there were 335 post-primary schools, that is, all classes above Standard IV, for Africans, 8 for Indians and 2 for Europeans. At the same time there were 1 699 lower primary schools for Africans, 90 for Indians and 24 for Europeans.

It was in January 1962[8] that all schools in Tanzania were fully integrated. Thus segregation ended and for the first time wise leadership gave to Tanzania the basic machinery required for creating a nation-wide educational system of a truly humane and non-racial kind.

The demand for education and training in Tanzania as independence approached was a result of a combination of factors. The need for large numbers of Africans with at least secondary education became obvious and the pressures for ex-

[6] United Nations: Social Reconstruction in the Newly Independent Countries of East Africa. New York, 1965. Social Welfare Services in Africa No. 4, p. 38.
[7] Schadler, Karl: Crafts, Small-scale Industries, and Industrial Education in Tanzania. London, C. Hurst & Co. 1968. Afrika-Studien Nr. 34, p. 113.
[8] Report of the Committee on the Integration of Education, 1959. Dar-es-Salaam 1960.

pansion mounted. Thus the most urgent need was for students who had completed secondary school, but the flow of secondary students required a larger out-turn from the primary schools. The primary schools were expanded rapidly, but the supply of teachers required for these schools absorbed most of the earlier primary-school leavers who should have gone to secondary schools.

For instance, the total enrolment figures increased from 400 000 in 1957 to over 800 000 in 1967 and between 1962 and 1967 Tanzania's primary-school leavers were more than 60 000.[9] Whereas in 1962 about one-third of the school-leavers (41 810) had a chance to be enrolled in a secondary school, it was not possible in 1967 for more than about 11 per cent in relative terms to enter secondary school. The almost 90 per cent who did not take the G.C.E. were faced with the problem of employment. What kinds of jobs could be created for the hundreds of thousands of 14-year-olds who were completing primary school and who had little prospect of continuing their education?

It has become common knowledge that by 1980 two-thirds of the population of the world will be under 20 years of age. In economic terms, this means that in a short ten years there will be 264 000 000 young people looking for jobs—most of them in the developing countries, most of them with scanty education or preparation but all with high and impatient expectations. Often only the shock of disappointment and frustration awaits them.[10]

From the employment point of view, this sudden expansion in primary-school enrolment posed an extremely dangerous socio-economic problem in terms of numbers alone.

From the foregoing, it is clear that an understanding of the educational problems bequeathed to Tanzania and to all other African countries by the colonial regime, with its threat to

---

[9] Tobias, G.: *High-Level Manpower Requirements and Resources in Tanganyika 1962–1967.* Government Paper No. 2 of 1963, Dar-es-Salaam, Government Printer, 1963, p. 9.

[10] Youth and Unemployment, in World Christian Education, Vol. 29, No. 1, 1970, p. 23. *Journal of the World Council of Christian Education,* Geneva 20, Switzerland.

impose crippling distortion on the entire educational, social, economic and political structure of the country, has no doubt guided President Nyerere and the TANU Government of Tanzania to seek new approaches in education for Tanzania. This is illustrated by the post-independence policies and goals of the government on education. The Three-year Plan for 1961–64, which laid emphasis on secondary education, called for a significant expansion on the secondary, especially the upper secondary, level and a cutback in planning expansion on the primary level, the extension of all primary-school courses to cover at least 6 years, because a 4-year education frequently did not result in permanent literacy, and also an increase in the local supply of trained teachers at the primary level as well as the secondary and university levels to replace foreigners on short-term assignments.

The main educational objectives of the Five-year Plan 1964–69 were to provide the high-level manpower needed for economic development, to maintain the quality of primary education at a level which would provide for permanent literacy and to attain qualitative and quantitative self-sufficiency in school teachers. The Plan pointed out that the percentage of the appropriate school-age population attending secondary school was so small that the continuation of this situation would entail a continued dependence upon foreign technicians and personnel to run the administrative and economic machinery of the country.

It is justifiable therefore for one to conclude that it was to remedy the present situation and to gear the output of the future to the needs of the economy that attempts were made in the first Five-year Plan to project the educational sector against the background of the situation in 1980—16 years ahead. The Plan anticipated that, except for some rare and highly specialized occupations, Tanzania would become self-sufficient in manpower in all economic fields and at all professional levels and that the shift in education programmes would be such as to match the number of school-leavers at the various levels of formal and technical education to the needs for manpower within the economy, without giving rise to a surplus of educated or semi-educated persons to aggravate the problems of unemployment. The implication therefore was that, at least until 1980, the main educational effort must go into equipping grown-ups to understand what the Development Plan is about, and to play an intelligent part in carrying out the social and economic changes called for by the Plan.

However, the formulator of the Plan admitted that the emphasis on economic needs might not be consistent, particularly at secondary and university levels, with views of education as a source of moral enrichment and aesthetic satisfaction or as the pursuit of pure learning.

It was financially impossible to provide education for all and such a mass education could be harmful to society as a whole when it was not accompanied by a simultaneous improvement of material living standards, together with commensurate employment opportunities. This was why President Nyerere in 1967 wrote:

Unpleasant though it may be, the fact is that it is going to be a long time before we can provide universal primary education in Tanzania. ... It is only a few who will have the chance of going on to secondary school ... [and] to university, even if they can benefit from doing so. These are the economic facts of life for our country. They are the practical meaning of our poverty.

The only choice before us is how we allocate the educational opportunities and whether we emphasize the individual interests of the few or whether we design our educational system to serve the community as a whole. And for a socialist state only the latter is really possible.

In April 1967 President Nyerere set forth in his white paper "Education for Self-Reliance" three changes which should be made in the educational system. A rise in school-entry age would make children older on completion of the primary-school course and thus better able to become immediately productive. Changes in the content of education would make each level complete in itself rather than a preparatory course for the next level. Emphasis was to be switched from preparation for examinations to preparation for the type of non-academic life most students would lead.

Secondly, to make the schools, especially at the secondary level, self-reliant parts of the economic and social community, each school would have a farm or workshop as an integral part of the institution; modern methods could be taught; and these forms would provide food for the community, as well as teach the students.

Thirdly, at the primary level children would be made integral participants in the local community. They would work on family or communal farms or on development projects in jobs commensurate with their health and strength; this experience would show them that education does not set one apart. Similarly, university and other higher-level students would be expected to participate during vacations in practical projects related to their fields of study, with part of their wages going to their college or institution.

In June 1967 the Minister for Education, Mr. Solomon Eliufoo, abolished boarding schools at the primary level, introduced the use of Swahili as the medium of instruction from the outset of primary school and English as a foreign language in the first year of school, instead in the third or fourth.

No history of education in Tanzania or in other African countries can be complete without a brief critique of the colonial educational policies and systems. President Nyerere's famous paper "Education for Self-Reliance" epitomizes the colonial educational legacy.

> The education provided by the colonial government was not designed to prepare young people for the service of their own country; instead, it was motivated by a desire to inculcate the value of the colonial society and to train individuals for the service of the colonial state. In these countries the state interest in education, therefore, stemmed from the need for local clerks and junior officials, it was modelled on the British system, but with even heavier emphasis on subservient attitudes and on white-collar skills.[12]

The same criticism of the unsuitable colonial educational system has been voiced out again recently by the Minister for National Education, Mr. C. Y. Mgonja. He bitterly commented that

---

[12] Nyerere, Julius K.: *Freedom and Socialism: Uhuru na Ujamaa*. Dar-es-Salaam, Oxford University Press, 1968, p. 269.

The colonialists were good at producing arrogant students who turned out to be exploiters and big bosses only.[13]

Furthermore, it could be seen too that the simple adoption of the European type of primary educational system necessarily involved serious consequences, putting a brake on social and economic progress by failing to prepare the pupils for grown-up tasks. It taught less than what was needed and also many things that were not of much avail to most Africans.

Also when it is remembered that the quality of education is often influenced by the cultural standard of the family and social environment of the pupils, that the parents and most grown-ups never went to school, that the housing and living conditions in most families are not suited for learning or doing homework, and that the value of learning is not placed very high, one cannot but admit the inevitability of introducing adult-literacy programmes.

It is also a well-known fact that in Tanzania, as well as in other African countries, school is almost the only source from which the new generation can acquire the fundamentals of knowledge and a more or less up-to-date cultural standard. The child who never gets there or abandons it too soon will have to depend on adult education for widening his knowledge and professional training.

A re-examination of the colonial educational system in Tanzania and in other African countries was therefore inevitable. The only logical answer was to gear the educational systems to the needs of each country and make them respond to those needs as each country developed and matured. There was need, too, to make the educational system respond to the changing patterns of needs and desires of Africa and the world at large, but its primary responsibility was that of meeting the needs of each country.

Convinced of this vital need for a new educational system, President Nyerere, in an address to the National Assembly on the Five-year Plan on 12 May 1964, said:

We cannot use our small resources on education for its own sake; we cannot even use them to make primary education available

[13] *The Nationalist of Tanzania,* 15 June 1970.

for all. Therefore we must educate adults. We cannot afford to wait for the children.

This same sentiment was expressed by the representative of the Director-General of the UNESCO at the opening of the adult-education conference at Abidjan in March 1964, when he said:

In any case, it is not the children of to-day who hold the present destiny of Africa in their hands, it is the adults. So it is only by establishing effective communication with the adult population, by helping them to adjust to a rapidly changing world, that an immediate impact can be made on the urgent problems of society and essential progress be brought about. Africa cannot wait a generation to mobilise its rich human resources for tasks of national development.[14]

Besides President Nyerere, Mr. C. Y. Mgonja and many other African leaders who take critical views of the educational policy of the colonial regime, Peter Mandi looks at the problem from the root cause and condemns the colonial educational-planning methods. He is of the opinion that only the method applied in making education plans by the Mediterranean countries, that of starting from the expected vocational structure to derive the tasks of education, in other words, having some relationship between profession (vocation) and schooling, can be regarded as planning procedure. He then argues:

In a physician's case it is clear that he needs university graduation, but what schooling must a shopkeeper, or the employees of the technological department in a factory, or a teacher have?[15]

President Nyerere's address to the workers at the May Day Rally in 1970 at Ilala sports stadium in Dar-es-Salaam seems to have supplied an answer to Peter Mandi's question. He said that it was untrue to think that one had to have a degree

[14] Widstrand, Carl Gösta (ed.): *Development and Adult Education in Africa.* Uppsala, The Scandinavian Institute of African Studies, 1965, p. 25.
[15] Mandi, Peter: *The Development of Education in Africa and Its Problems.* Studies in Developing Countries Series. Centre for Afro-Asian Research of the Hungarian Academy of Sciences. Budapest, 1969, p. 13.

before one could become a manager, although it was equally untrue that leaders of industry could just be picked up off the street. What was needed, he continued, was an understanding of the operation of the industry and warned his audience that workers had to be ready to educate themselves.[16]

The development and progress of adult education in Tanzania

The preceding discussion of the history of formal education in Tanzania places the development of adult education in its proper perspective. The shortcomings of the colonial educational system, especially their effect on the production of trained manpower and the economic, social and political development of the country, can be regarded as one of the causes of the critical attitude of the leaders of this country and, in fact, most African leaders. It was the need to bring about certain changes in the post-Independence educational policy of Tanzania that led to the search for other alternatives. Adult education was readily accepted as the inevitable alternative.

The prime objectives of adult education in Tanzania were clearly outlined by President Nyerere in his 1970 New Year broadcast to the nation. He spelt out the objectives as being:

1. To shake ourselves out of a resignation to the kind of life Tanzanian people have lived for centuries past. "The first job of adult education will be to make us reject bad houses, bad *jembes*, and preventable diseases; it will make us recognise that we ourselves have the ability to obtain better houses, better tools, and better health."

2. To learn how to improve our lives. "We have to learn how to produce more on our farms, about better food ... about modern methods of hygiene and how to work together to improve the conditions in our villages and streets."

---

[16] *The Standard of Tanzania,* 2 May 1970, p. 1: "Workers to move into management. It was time that the managers of Tanzania's industries came from the ranks of the workers themselves."

3. To understand our national policies of socialism and self-reliance. "We must learn about the plans for national economic advances, so that we can ensure that we all play our part in making them a success and that we all benefit from them."[17]

Before concluding the broadcast, President Nyerere said that the TANU and the Government were preparing plans to give emphasis to adult education and to make the people's efforts in this field more effective and that the TANU Central Committee at its last meeting had approved the broad policies of an adult-education programme, which would be announced in due course.

The Adult Education Section in the Second Five-year Plan for Economic and Social Development, July 1969 to 30 June 1974 (volume 1, pages 157 and 158), states that the main emphasis in adult education in this Plan period will be on rural development. This will include simple training in agricultural techniques and craftsmanship, health education, housecraft, simple economics and accounting, and education in politics and the responsibilities of the citizens. In rural areas virtually the whole of this work will be conducted in Swahili and literacy will be included in response to popular demand, as people become aware of its functional importance.

The Plan assumes the needs of urban areas may be met in part by existing organizations, notably the University Institute of Adult Education, but leaves room for the expansion of simple vocational classes, for which provision is not made by existing training institutions.

The development proposals in the Plan place the main organising responsibility on the primary school. The school will become a community educational centre, at which the provision of primary education is only one function. A school so conceived will increasingly become a focal point for the total educational needs of the community, rather than serving as a somewhat detached institution for the education of children. According to the Plan, the general responsibility for the adult-education activities of the centre will rest with the head-

[17] *The Nationalist of Tanzania,* 1 January 1970, p. 1: "1970 Adult Education Year—Nyerere."

master. It will be the duty of the headmaster to ascertain community needs, to identify suitable instructors and to arrange classes. Each headmaster will have at his disposal a small grant for equipment and materials.

Instruction will be given by persons supplied by Ministries and organisations or by individuals in the neighbourhood who are competent to give instruction. The Institute of Adult Education will assist the programme by providing training for the corps of education officers who will provide leadership for its development. In addition to conducting research and experimentation in adult education, it is envisaged that the Institute will carry out a pilot project aimed at the establishment of a National Correspondence College to serve literate but isolated persons throughout the country, who wish to enlarge their knowledge and understanding, particularly in subjects of importance to national development.

The Minister for National Education, Mr. C. Y. Mgonja, has recently explained what "appropriate and practical steps"[18] have so far been taken to implement the Plan for Adult Education. These include the formation of a programme for committees that will deal with adult education from national level to the regional, district, divisional and village levels; training special officers to organise adult education in the districts; organising courses for teachers and all other people concerned with adult education to orient them in the methods of teaching adults and the provision of a special budget for adult education. Furthermore, efforts are being made to provide each District Adult Education Organiser with a Landrover to enable him to travel around to perform his duties.

Commenting on the role of the University of Dar-es-Salaam[19] in the campaign for adult education in the country, the Minister said that the University Institute of Adult Education is fully committed.

---

[18] *The Nationalist of Tanzania*, 15 June 1970, p. 4: "The Minister for National Education, Mr. C. Y. Mgonja, talks to our staff writer on the question of adult education: Plan for adult education."
[19] The University of Dar-es-Salaam was founded on 1 July 1970 and was formally inaugurated on 29 August 1970.

(a) *The Institute of Adult Education*

The history of adult education in Tanzania dates back to the late 1940's, when adult education was associated with community development. From 1946 to 1949 the Social Welfare Organisation which championed the cause directed its efforts mainly to literacy campaigns. The ex-servicemen in welfare centres in towns needed adult education for literacy. The Social Welfare Organisation became a Department in 1949 (the Social Department), and its functions increased to include youth clubs. After Independence in 1961 more community workers were appointed to carry out adult education in rural areas. In 1964 the Institute of Adult Education was established by the Council of the University College in exercise of the powers conferred by Section 5, sub-section 3 (*b*) of the University College, Dar-es-Salaam, Act, 1963. The Institute grew out of a Department of Extra-Mural Studies which had been set up in Tanzania soon after the establishment of the University College. Previous to that, university adult education in the country had been provided, on a much smaller scale, under the auspices of the Extra-Mural Department of University College, Makerere, Uganda.

The activities of the Institute of Adult Education are as varied as the aims. In Dar-es-Salaam, most of the Institute's activities are at present concentrated at the University Adult Education Centre in Lumumba Street.[20] The activities range from providing courses for adults, professional training for teachers of adults and administrators engaged in adult education, and library facilities for adult educators to collecting and disseminating information on adult education and conducting research and experiment in adult education, in addition to the Institute's pilot projects on radio education and the establishment of a National Correspondence Institute. In consultation with national movements, ministries, students and its Council, in an effort to offer courses which meet needs for national development as well as individual growth, the Insti-

[20] The Centre, a four-storey building, was the old home of the University College until 1961, when the College moved to its present site eight miles from the town.

tute, over the past few years, has offered courses in the following fields: economics, government, international relations, rural development, history, law, management, languages, effective writing, public speaking, psychology, sociology, philosophy, art, music and drama. The teaching staff consists of the Institute staff and part-time tutors, largely from the University, government and semi-official bodies. A University College Certificate Course in Law, offered primarily to civil servants who need some knowledge of law in their work, was started in July 1968. A nine-month residential Diploma Course in Adult Education began in July 1969, with 23 candidates from various ministries and organisations.

Among the training courses for teachers of adults, which have also been conducted, often in co-operation with government bodies or national movements, are an 11-week course for the Tanzania People's Defence Force (TPDF) and National Service teachers of adults; two-week courses for literacy teachers in co-operation with the Ministry of Rural Development; evening classes for teachers of adults in community centres, a seminar for co-operative education secretaries, and two-week training courses for teachers of adults as part of the the East African Seminars.

To collect and disseminate information on adult education, the Institute has prepared and issued a Directory of Adult Education Agencies and Courses in Tanzania, a Handbook for Adult Education Associations (issued in both English and Swahili versions), and a Directory of Lectures offered by University staff. It has also started on a handbook for adult students preparing for mature-age entry to the University, approved by the Council of the Institute.

In its area of research and experiment in adult education, the Institute has made simple analyses of the student population and trends from term to term. In tackling the problem of why students drop out of classes, a problem in adult education throughout the world, a study has been made and is now being summarised. This study will provide information on student motivation and offer a basis for future planning.

A pilot project on radio education, emphasizing the use of radio listening groups, was conducted in the Southern Region, with written materials provided for the use of these groups. The findings and evaluation of this project will serve as a guide to the future radio education activities of the Institute. A tutor has been assigned full-time to radio education and the Institute will offer radio courses, as well as assist in forming radio learning groups, training group leaders, providing study guides and evaluating results. There is a need, too, for measurement of the extent of listening to educational broadcasts, as well as their effectiveness.

A pilot project on the effectiveness of study groups in teaching basic economics has been started and will involve the preparation of study guides and visual aids, organising study groups, training group leaders, evaluating the effectiveness of these groups, and revising the programme of the basis of this experiment. It is hoped that this pilot project may produce results which can point the way to an effective means of reaching large numbers of people throughout the country.

An application for technical and financial assistance has been forwarded to the Swedish International Development Authority for the establishment of a National Correspondence Study Institute. If granted, and if the Institute opens its door to students, it will serve the total correspondence-study needs of the country.

The Institute has three regional centres in Mbeya, Moshi and Mwanza, in addition to the headquarters in Dar-es-Salaam. The functions of the regional centres are to determine the adult-education needs in the area which can be met by the Institute; to organise and conduct adult classes, residential seminars, and other educational activities; to offer professional training for teachers of adults; and to provide counselling to adult students, including mature-age-entry candidates. These regional centres will continue to assist others with their programmes of adult education and might well become centres where all of those engaged in adult education could come for assistance on teaching methods, course organisation, and teaching aids.

(b) Kivukoni College

Besides the Institute of Adult Education, Kivukoni College in Dar-es-Salaam has become a centre for political education and leadership training in Tanzania and for the continuing education of adults.

Kivukoni College is an example of a residential college. It was opened in July 1961 by the Chairman of the Tanganyika Education Trust Fund, Mwalimu Julius K. Nyerere, then Prime Minister of Tanganyika. At the opening ceremony Mwalimu said:

> This College is a practical demonstration of what can be done by the determined effect of the people of this country. It is *our* College; the people of Tanganyika have provided all the money which has been spent on it up to now; they have created it, determined its shape, and will govern it.[21]

In 1961 and 1969, the College had 39 and 127 students respectively for the long and short courses. The long-course students include people from the Tanganyika African National Union (TANU), the National Union of Tanganyika Workers (NUTA), the Tanzania Peoples' Defence Force (TPDF), the TANU Youth League (TYL) and Umoja wa Wanawake wa Tanzania (UWT), as well as rural development assistants, school teachers, National Service-men, clerks and farmers. The short courses cater for primary court magistrates and probation and welfare workers.

A three-month-long seminar[22] was conducted at the College at the beginning of the year. It was attended by 60 District Education Officers (Adult Education).

The Work-oriented Literacy Project, launched in 1967 on a Five-year Plan basis, has been extended for one extra year to 1972. The Project is jointly run by the United Nations Educational, Scientific and Cultural Organisation (UNESCO) and the Tanzanian Government.

There is a Tanzanian Literacy Campaign Committee. One

---

[21] Nyerere, J. K.: *Freedom and Unity*. Dar-es-Salaam. Oxford University Press, 1967, pp. 119 ff.
[22] Konde, Hadji: Self-reliance at Kivukoni College. *The Standard of Tanzania*, 2 April 1970, p. 4.

of the aims of the Campaign Committee is to produce 75 000 new literates before the end of the Plan period in 1972 and also to achieve the complete eradication of illiteracy in Ukerewe Island by the end of 1971. The Committee administers pilot literacy projects in the Mwanza and Shinyanga regions at a total cost of Shs. 42 000 000.

A meeting of the Tanzanian Literacy Campaign Committee was held at Mwanza on 22 August 1970, to review matters related to adult-education policy. The meeting also discussed such issues as functional teaching and reading materials, as well as the use of visual aids for literacy classes.

The plans for this year include running 1 500 literacy classes with about 35 000 adult students. Next year an additional 2 500 classes to accommodate about 60 000 are planned (*Sunday News,* 23 August 1970, p. 5).

The turn-out for adult-education classes during the months of May, June and July in the pilot areas of Busega, Nansio, Negedi and Ihangiro is reported to be about 20 045, including 13 000 women.

In this year's expansion programme it is intended that the ever-increasing *ujamaa* villages in the four regions will be covered by the literacy campaign. The project will also undertake to supply teaching materials in the literacy centres. The project has already trained 1 199 functional literacy educators.

The National Service is also making a great contribution to adult education. Enlisted men and women spend a good part of their time in the National Service helping to teach literacy classes along with primary- and secondary-school teachers. Extensive use is made of secondary-school students as well, and this year's provision of 44 Land Rovers, in addition to film vans, should help in easing the transport difficulties that are always encountered in attempts to reach distant villages.

This section would be incomplete without mentioning the other types of adult education and the agencies providing it. The following are some of the kinds of adult education being provided in Tanzania, and the organisations which provide it.

Almost every Ministry provides some kind of adult education, including Agriculture, Food and Cooperatives (extension work, farmers' training centres), Health (extension work, health centres), Rural Development (rural development workers, district training centres), Education (responsible for adult education in Tanzania, including direct responsibility for literacy and evening classes for adults), Central Establishments Division (civil-service training centre and other training programmes for civil servants), Police, Prisons, the Tanzania Peoples' Defence Force, Information (Radio Tanzania), Communications and Works (including the National Institute of Productivity).

The national organisations include the TANU for political education, the NUTA for workers' education, the UWT for education for women, the CUT for cooperative education, the TAPA for education for parents, and the TYL, some of whose educational programmes are directed to adults.

Employers provide in-service training for workers, both formal and on-the-job. Voluntary organisations include the YWCA, the YMCA, the Red Cross, Churches and religious organisations and the Tanzania Society for the Prevention of Cruelty to Animals (TSPCA).

Thus in speaking of "Adult Education in Tanzania", all of the above, and others, are included.

According to the latest figures released by the Directorate of Adult Education of the Ministry of National Education, over 200 000 people throughout mainland Tanzania are participating in adult-education classes. Altogether, since April this year, 250 343 adults have registered themselves for different courses under the auspices of the Directorate of Adult Education, which was set up early this year to co-ordinate adult-education activities in the country hitherto undertaken by several largely unco-ordinated bodies.

The report also indicates that there has already been a significant upsurge of interest among the people in ridding themselves of illiteracy and ignorance.

Available statistics from 10 regions which submitted progress reports on adult-education programmes for the month of May had shown that 54 163 people enrolled themselves for adult-education courses. Returns from seven other regions, namely, Dodoma, Mara, Mwanza, Ruvuma, Kigoma, Shinyanga and Tabora, were not available to the Ministry of National Education headquarters in Dar-es-Salaam at the time of writing this paper.

Of the 10 regions, Mbeya topped the list by recording the highest enrolment figure of 22 554. Figures for the other regions were as follows: Arusha (2 294); Coast (547); Iringa (6 600); Kilimanjaro (5 598); Morogoro (298), Mtwara (7 168); Singida (1 468); Tanga (2 709) and West Lake (4 927).

It is significant that, of the total figure for the people who enrolled during the period under review, the number of women exceeded that of men by more than 10 000. There were 76 010 women, as against only 65 133 men during the month of June (*The Nationalist of Tanzania*, 22 August 1970, p. 1).

Furthermore, the progress report showed that more people were enrolling for lessons on how to read and write than any other courses offered through the scheme.

Altogether 12 different courses are offered under the adult education programme. These include lessons on how to read and write; home economics and handicrafts; the basic elements of health and hygiene; languages; commercial subjects and above all, political education, with emphasis on the country's policy of *ujamaa* and its implications for the people of Tanzania. In May this year a total of 57 763 adults attended home-economics and home-craft classes.

The Assistant Director of National Education (Adult Education), Mr. A. S. Sajine, revealed during an interview that the enrolment of adults has expanded "so much so that our Directorate has not been able to cope with the growing demands for reading material and other stationery". Mr. Sajine attributed the "big rush" for adult education to the political consciousness among the people and added: "It is also a visible sign of the way in which the people have responded well to Mwalimu's call."

The role of libraries in adult education in Tanzania

If the Institute of Adult Education and all the other agencies and organisations providing adult education are the activists in the total plan of adult education in Tanzania, then the libraries, especially the public libraries and the University Library, can be regarded as the catalysts, because education, whether primary, secondary, college, university or adult, implies books and means whereby books can be made available and accessible. Though much adult education can be done without books, for example, education by radio, by some discussion groups, and by extension workers giving demonstrations, libraries not only provide books but preserve the results of educational work already done.

(a) The Tanganyika Library Services

The Tanganyika Library Services Board was established by an Act of Parliament, the Tanganyika Library Services Board Act, 1963, "... to promote, establish, equip, manage, maintain and develop libraries in Tanganyika ...".[23]

In accordance with this Act, the Tanganyika Library Services Board has established efficient public libraries at Dar-es-Salaam, Tanga, Mwanza, Iringa, Bukoba and Kibaha, with Korogwe and Moshi as new additional centres. According to the Library Statistics for December 1969, the Dar-es-Salaam Central Library has a total of 69 189 volumes and serves 7 707 registered readers; Tanga 17 958 volumes and 3 329 readers, Mwanza 14 717 volumes and 3 379 readers, Iringa 11 077 volumes and 1 704 readers; Bukoba 7 379 volumes and 828 readers; Kibaha and Moshi have 14 484 and 10 394 volumes respectively.

There is a postal library service designed for readers in main-land Tanganyika who live in places without library facilities. A book-box service also exists for schools, colleges and communities such as hospitals, prisons and community centres. The Mwanza Rural Library serves the Kongoe and Noko Primary Schools, the Kongoe dispensary, the sisal estate and the Soga village, while the Kibaha Rural Library serves the Kibaha Primary School and the surrounding communities.

---

[23] The Tanganyika Library Services Board Act, 1963, No. 39 of 1963. Subsidiary legislation in the Tanganyika Library Services Board Regulations 1964.

The new programme to cover the next Five-year National Development Plan[24] comprises work in the fields of school, rural and special library development and the streamlining of the branch-library development programme to allow it to proceed at a fairly rapid pace. The Tanganyika Library Service plans to tackle the task of urban development by reducing or confining its building programmes to the major population centres, such as Tabora, Morogoro, Mtwara, Moshi and possibly Mbeya. Libraries for towns like Lindi, Kigoma and Musoma will have to be deferred or development confined to the inexpensive adaptation of existing premises financed largely by grants from local authorities.

The rural library services place emphasis on the expansion of the library service into the more remote areas of the countryside, based on the branch libraries established in towns. The success of this programme will greatly depend on the provision of mobile services to scattered settlements within easy access of well-established and well-surfaced all-weather roads, and secondly the provision of some form of service to large isolated villages. Two mobile libraries which will be presented by the German Government are expected to arrive in Tanzania in September and will serve the Mwanza and Tanga Rural Libraries respectively. Some form of static service point, providing not only the place to house a collection of books but also space for study and reading will be adequate for the large isolated villages. There will also be a combined library and adult literacy centre, under the control of an assistant trained in basic library skills, in the Mwanza Group Library area, in co-operation with the UNESCO Adult Literacy Project.

Special library development at the present time includes two schemes, namely, the Commercial and Financial Informa-

---

[24] (a) Tanganyika Library Services Board, 12 March 1970. Memorandum by the Director on the Draft Estimates for the year ending 30 June 1971. (b) *The Nationalist of Tanzania*, 26 May 1970, p. 3: "Tanganyika Library Service", interview with the Director (T.L.S.), Mr. E. M. Broome.

tion Service based on the Bank of Tanzania and the National Development Corporation and, secondly, the Technical Information Service based on the Dar-es-Salaam Technical College. The NDC already enjoys the efficient service of a trained librarian and has a collection of over 1 000 books and 70 periodicals.

A National Bibliography is in preparation and the 1969 volume, with about 270 entries, is nearing completion. The 1964–68 cumulation will be published later. Cards for books and periodicals before 1964 are being prepared too.

The School Library Service development programme sponsored by the UNESCO has already started with the establishment of a model service in three schools—the Mzumbe Government Secondary School (3 500 books), the Iringa Girls Secondary School (500 books) and the Alliance Secondary School in Dodoma (12 000 books). These school libraries will serve a dual purpose. They will be used as training centres for the teachers in these three regions, so that the schools will make full and effective use of the books that they will receive as loan collections from the Library Service.

Colleges with fairly good libraries include the College of National Education and the Technical College in Dar-es-Salaam, the Colleges of National Education in Marangu, Butimba, Mwanza and Morogoro, the Co-operative College at Moshi, and the College of African Wildlife Management in Mwika.

The Tanganyika Library Services Board is also co-operating with the Directorate of Adult Education and has plans for specially selected collections of books to be despatched to the 60 newly appointed district adult-education officers who will be responsible for lending them to the villages which they visit in the course of their work.

The Board is not unaware of the future library needs of the fast-growing number of *ujamaa* villages. Meanwhile villagers, especially around Mwanza, are being persuaded to provide suitable accommodation on a self-help basis. It is hoped too that, when plans for schools in *ujamaa* villages are being considered, accommodation for small libraries and reading rooms may be incorporated.

(b) *The University Library, Dar-es-Salaam*

Besides the Tanganyika Library Service Board, the University Library also makes important contributions to adult education in Tanzania. The primary issue to examine here is not the educational role of the University Library but the role of the University itself in adult education. The University Library is essentially a service department whose obligation is first to the University and whose main function is to organise and develop the teaching and research materials of the University. If the Faculty may be compared to the brain of the University, it is equally true that its Library resembles a powerful heart, sending the life-blood of learning through the whole University body, nourishing every part of it and enabling it draw strength from accumulated thought. Nevertheless the University recognizes its responsibilities to adult education and its obligation to give continuing service to adult students.

The establishment of the Institute of Adult Education in accordance with the provisions of the University College, Dar-es-Salaam, Act, 1963, marked the beginning of that recognition. Under its decrees, one of the four aims of the Institute of Adult Education is to provide advisory services and library facilities for adult educators, including the dissemination of information about adult education.

The Institute has developed a library on adult education, distinct from its book collections for students, for the use of all adult educators. The subject fields covered by these book collections include the organisation and administration of adult education, methods and techniques for teaching adults, visual aids, research in adult education, community development, and handbooks prepared for adult education in Tanzania, as well as adult-education periodicals, catalogues and bulletins from a number of countries. It is proposed to expand the Institute Library collections on adult education both in Dar-es-Salaam and the regions. There is increased emphasis on training in adult education and advisory service.

It is uneconomical for the Institute to aim at building a book collection covering a variety of subject fields, since the Tanganyika Library Service and the University Library are already meeting many of the needs of the adult students, both in Dar-es-Salaam and in up-country centres. The University Library collection in December 1969 was 120 000 volumes, including 15 000 in the Law collection, and over 2 400 current periodical titles. The Library is also the National Depository for Tanzania under the Libraries (Deposit of Books) Act of 1962 and receives the publications of major international organisations, such as the United Nations. The East Africana collection consists of specialized research facilities on East Africa and Africa generally and could therefore be the foundation of a National Documentation Centre for Tanzania. There are also government documents and other special materials, such as manuscripts, maps and microfilms. The Main Library has two new branch libraries at Muhimbili and Morogoro for the Faculties of Medicine and Agriculture. The Medical and Agricultural Libraries have over 10 000 and 8 000 volumes respectively. A third branch library will be founded with the establishment of a Faculty of Engineering in 1972.

The Library resources are freely available to all full-time students and staff of the University. The Library Regulations extend facilities to non-University readers for reference and research upon the presentation of satisfactory identification. The current record of registered readers shows a total of over 2 500, including 160 non-University borrowers. The Library also extends its services in the form of inter-library loans, by telephone and mail. The High Court of Tanzania and a number of other government ministries and organisations receive a regular telephone-enquiry service from the University Library. There are no barriers to the use of books. The Library maintains an open-shelf policy and, furthermore, readers' seats are arranged close to the book-shelves. The Reserve Shelve Section ensures the greatest use by the greatest number of students of the reading materials recommended by the teaching staff.

Some of the most valuable contributions made to adult education by the University Library are the services of the Bindery, Printing and Photographic Units. The Bindery not only serves the University Library but also undertakes jobs from the various departments and faculties, institutes and bureaux, in addition to a number of government departments and also the Institute of Adult Education. According to the 1969 statistics, the Bindery Unit produced 2 586 full bindings, 6 198 flush bindings, 14 848 booklets and pads, and 17 766 manilla sides and cloth spines.

The Photographic Unit works for the Library and all faculties and institutes of the University. It also serves the National Museum and National Archives. The Printing Unit serves all departments, faculties, and some government departments. It prints stationery, bulletins, invoice books, invitation cards, magazines and even pamphlets. According to the 1969 records, the Photographic Unit produced 8 267 photographic enlargements, 54 968 microfilm exposures (negatives), 101 857 microfilm prints (positives), and 63 883 photocopies, while the Printing Unit produced 1 244 535 printing (offset) impressions. The most recent productions of the Printing Unit include 1 000 copies of the *Darlite Magazine* for the Department of Languages and Linguistics, 2 000 copies of the *Uchumi* magazine for the Economic Society of Tanzania, 1 000 copies of *Inawezekana* for the Katoke Teacher Training Centre, 3 500 copies of the Secondary School Physics Data Book for the Institute of Education, 1 000 copies of the Swahili Legal Terms Dictionary for the Faculty of Law, 1 000 copies of Paper of Hans Cory Books, and also 1 000 copies of the District Data Books for the Ministry of Economic Affairs. These publications are read by both adult educators and adult students.

Another indirect contribution of the Library to adult education is the stimulation of interest and the generation of a healthy habit of reading and a desire for books. The numerous library exhibitions and frequent displays of books donated by foreign embassies and important personalities draw steady streams of sightseers as well as serious students.

The general public visits the Library on open days. Lectures and concerts of the highest quality are regular features of the educational programmes of the University. Conferences and seminars enjoy a suitable environment in the University. Learned societies, including the East African Academy and the Tanzania Society, make use of the Library.

Problems of adult education and libraries

It is a well-known fact that, once a country decides to take seriously the educational needs of its adults, it is immediately faced with a number of problems. The case of Tanzania is therefore not an exception. The problems facing adult education in Tanzania are many and varied. They range from finance, shortage of trained personnel, lack of teachers and reading materials, student drop-out, fear of the literates relapsing into illiteracy and maintenance of the enthusiasm of the learning adults to the improvement of the low standard of written and spoken Swahili.

Since Independence there has been a growing recognition by the national leaders of what can be achieved through the existing adult-education agencies. The response of the adults has been so positive and impressive that the leaders of this country are satisfied that the policy of educating adults is right. The leaders are also aware that this revolution in education, with the resultant revolutionary spirit, is a sign of progress which is bound to cause problems. Therefore the problems enumerated above were anticipated.

The TANU Government of Tanzania is tackling each of these problems. Finance is more or less the common denominator. The Ministry of National Education is putting up a case for a special budget on adult education amounting to Shs. 9 000 000 for recurrent expenditure and over Shs. 2 000 000 for capital expenditure. A plan for the extension of the Home Economics Training Centre at Musoma was signed in Dar-es-Salaam on 18 June 1970 between the United Nations Development Programme and the Government of Tanzania. The estimated cost of the proposed extension of the project will amount to Shs. 3 244 801. Other contributions in experts, local staff and labour, buildings, equipment supplies and other facilities will amount to Shs. 802 574.

Also the Lutheran Church in Tanzania is planning to build churches and schools in *ujamaa* villages and to provide medical and social services. According to the Director of the Moshi-based Lutheran Radio Centre, the Rev. K. E. Amos Lyimo, the Lutheran Church at the moment is building a Shs.

6 000 000 secondary school in Mbulu District as part of the work of the Church in the current Five-year Development Plan. These facilities will also be used by adult educators.

There is also the problem of inadequate teachers and organisers. Here, too, the Government is proving equal to the task. District Education (Adult Education) Officers in the districts and the Institute of Adult Education staff are at the moment very much engaged in training the teachers of adult education of all types through weekend seminars and residential seminars before they teach. It is worth mentioning here that Mrs. Maria Nyerere, the wife of the President, after going through a short course in adult education, said that "she intends to tackle the illiteracy war with a slightly new approach, aiming at making her students literate within three months instead of the usual six-month period", adding, "but I shall keep everything within the policy".[25] She opened a new phase in the war against illiteracy when she started teaching an adult-education class at Magomeni Community Centre in Dar-es-Salaam. Furthermore, the projected Mwanza Radio Station to be established with the help of the UNESCO will train adult-education teachers and teach adults who enrol themselves. It must be mentioned, too, that Tanzania is to spend a total of Shs. 26 000 000 on training teachers under its plan of education for self-reliance by 1975. In announcing this education plan, the Minister for National Education, Mr. C. Y. Mgonja, thanked the UNICEF and the UNESCO for their contribution of Shs. 8 000 000 towards the training programme.

The Ministry of National Education (Adult Education) on 29 June 1970 issued a circular entitled "Adult Education (Illiteracy Campaign)" to all Regional Education Officers. This circular is an important government policy statement, announcing the programme for the celebration of the 10th Uhuru Anniversary next year.

According to the circular, the following decisions have been made:

---

[25] (*a*) *The Nationalist of Tanzania,* 24 May 1970, p. 1: "Mile-stone set in literacy campaign". (*b*) *The Standard of Tanzania,* 24 May 1970.

(*a*) Special arrangements are to be made to declare certain areas in Tanzania as being free from illiteracy. These areas include the islands of Ukerewe, Ukara, and Mafia.

(*b*) Apart from the above areas, every region must endeavour to have one special zone in which much emphasis should be placed, so that every person in that zone should know how to read and write before 9 December 1971. Every Regional Education Officer is asked to contact his District Education Officers and Committees of Adult Education, so that arrangements may be made to declare those areas as being free from illiteracy.

(*c*) Areas such as islands and villages on valleys and hills that can be easily identified for geographical reasons are to be selected for further examination.

(*d*) The following areas are to be carefully selected:

(i) Populated areas.

(ii) Where residents have the will to educate themselves.

(iii) Where there are government and TANU Officials who have the will to progress.

(iv) Where adult-education centres are available (such places as TANU offices, schools, courts, welfare centres, etc.).

(v) Where teachers for adult education are available.

This work is expected to start immediately with the compilation of the following data:

(i)   Number of residents, i.e. population.
(ii) Number of those who cannot read and write.
(iii) Number of primary, secondary and higher schools.
(iv) Number of other centres to be used.
(v)   Number of centres that need to be opened.
(vi) Number of text-books needed.
(vii) Number of slice-boards needed.
(viii) Number of volunteer teachers needed.

To enable *ujamaa* villagers to become free from illiteracy, their villages are to be included in the different places that may be selected.

The campaign was officially launched on 16 July 1970, when some copies of the booklets entitled *Uchaguzi ni Wako* (Your Election) were presented to the Speaker of the National Assembly, Chief Adam Sapi, by the Director, Mr. Mhaiki.[26] The

---

[26] *The Standard of Tanzania*, 17 July 1970, p. 1: "Campaign for education on election".

64-page booklets, which examine the history of elections in Tanzania, make one item in the study campaign, which consists of a series of 10 radio programmes on Radio Tanzania, Swahili Service. Also included are visual aids, and hints to group-leaders.

The booklets outline the duties and responsibilities of the President, the National Assembly, and local government councils and how the elections will be carried out. They will be distributed to all District Adult Education Officers of the Ministry of National Education and the Institute of Adult Education's resident tutors who are organising the study groups all over the country. These booklets are expected to be used by adult study groups all over the country for learning more about Tanzania's election system.

International Literacy Day, 8 September 1970, and the Adult Education Week were also celebrated in September. The Director of National Education issued a circular on 1 July 1970 to all Regional Education Officers, District Education Officers (Adult Education), headmasters of secondary schools and principals of teacher-training colleges, Regional Commissioners and Area Commissioners, announcing plans for the celebration of the Adult Education Week (2–8 September 1970).

According to the circular, International Literacy Day was to be celebrated throughout the world in a variety of ways. In Tanzania, there were to be processions, *ngoma* dances, and speech-making by leaders. Two main projects were also to be undertaken during the week. These were fund-raising campaigns and advertising all the adult-education programmes which have been successfully carried out in Tanzania.

The problem of drop-outs in adult education centres is a universal one. The government is aware of this and many efforts are being made to train the teachers in the methods of teaching adults and to make sure that the content is practical and useful to the adults. The political leaders know that the attendance of adults is very much influenced by the encouragement and motivation they can get from them and therefore the TANU leaders all over the country take keen interest in adult classes in their areas.

All the various organisations are represented on the National

Advisory Council on Adult Education. They are represented in the sub-committees and the regional, district, divisional and village adult-education committees, with the specific aim of involving them in making the policy, so that they can readily help in implementing it.

It is the policy of the government to provide facilities for the educated people to continue learning even after school and to further improve themselves. The National Correspondence Study Institute is one of these facilities. It is also planned to revive evening classes in all the regional towns and to start new ones where they do not exist. Various ministries are encouraging the literates to learn more. For instance, the National Union of Tanganyika Workers (NUTA) further expanded its education programme during 1969, in order to acquaint the workers with the relevant knowledge of the development of the country's economy. During 1969, the NUTA, with the co-operation of the National Institute for Productivity, organised eight seminars for members of the workers' committees, at which 1 093 workers' representatives attended. Nine workers attended six-month courses at Kivukoni College, while other workers took various other courses at the University College, Dar-es-Salaam, and abroad, including East and West Germany, the Soviet Union, Romania, Bulgaria, the United Arab Republic and Great Britain.[27]

The government also plans to continue the system of sending Members of Parliament to the University of Dar-es-Salaam for short courses. Announcing this in Parliament on Saturday, 20 June 1970, the Parliamentary Secretary in the Second Vice-President's Office, Mr. F. V. Mponji, said that courses like the one conducted from 17 to 24 September 1969, for some Members of Parliament, especially the courses in economics, had proved very valuable and would continue in future.

The newly acquired literacy must be made functional. The government intends to establish centres for giving demonstrations of ox-driven farming implements in each district and *ujamaa* village where such implements can be utilised and to

---

[27] The NUTA 1969 Report presented to the TANU National Executive Committee.

initiate mobile training and demonstration units, which will make tours to *ujamaa* villages to show the peasants how to use modern farming implements. Announcing this in Parliament on 16 June 1970, during question time, the Minister for Agriculture, Food and Co-operatives, Mr. Derek Bryceson, said that, during the Second Five-year Development Plan, the government has placed special emphasis on stepping up the activities of the Tanganyika Machinery Testing Unit (TAMTU), which was already manufacturing ox-driven ploughs, seed-sowing machines, trailers, water-pumping machines for irrigation and groundnut harvesters.

He added that there were already 20 centres for training oxen and donkeys in the Kigoma, Mbeya, Singida, Kilimanjaro, Arusha, Mara, Tabora, Shinyanga, West Lake and Coast Regions and that peasants were already training their oxen and donkeys themselves in Ufipa, Tabora, Singida, Mara and Arusha.

Last but not the least in importance is the problem of the poor standard of spoken and written Swahili. There should be a constant improvement in the standard of Swahili and the translation into Swahili of books in foreign languages should become a major industry.

The nation-wide campaign to educate people in the importance of using the Kiswahili language is a step in the right direction. Mr. Ntiro, the Commissioner for Culture, has urged the National Council for Kiswahili to strive hard in this campaign to convince the people that a national language is very important to the nation. Addressing members of the National Kiswahili Council when he opened the Council's five-day meeting at the University College, Dar-es-Salaam (5–10 June), the Second Vice-President, Mr. Rashidi Kawawa, said that "the sovereignty of Tanzania cannot be complete unless the peasants and workers of this country identify themselves with the national language, which is Kiswahili".

More research in Swahili is vital. The Institute of Swahili Research at the University has this task as its special responsibility. Mr. George A. Mhina, the Acting Director of the Institute, is actively and enthusiastically encouraging research projects. One of the Research Fellows, Mr. J. A. Tejani, is currently working on a Swahili/Swahili Dictionary and also revising a standard Swahili-English Dictionary published by the Oxford University Press in 1939.

Libraries in Tanzania have almost identical problems. Lack of funds affects development programmes and training schemes. For instance, the Bank of Tanzania and the East African Institute of Malaria and Vector-borne Diseases are anxious to have well-organised libraries, but there is a shortage of funds and trained librarians.

Financing library development, like adult education, constitutes a problem on many different levels and requires large input components, which international financial aid might well introduce. Educational aid, including library development, in the form of the unilateral transfer of sums of money without any strings or earmarks for easily identifiable prestige projects, ought to be given to countries like Tanzania, which are careful in their financial planning. The UNESCO is already assisting but could perhaps increase its aid. The Rockefeller, Carnegie and Ford Foundations, which have the wherewithal to help, are hereby called upon to assist. All friendly governments should also aid generously.

The challenge of adult education to libraries in Tanzania

The Tanzania Library Association has the duty to provide the direction for library action. In response to the Presidential call, the Association should devote its 1970 Annual General Conference to Adult Education to the theme "Library and Adult Education in Tanzania: Present and Future Trends". Delegates to the Conference should include not only librarians, publishers and booksellers but members of other national organisations and agencies concerned with adult education. The Adult Education Association, the Council of the Institute of Adult Education, the Institutes of Education and Swahili Research at the University and the Ministries of National Education, Community Development and National Culture ought to be invited to send representatives. National corporations and trade unions, including the Tanganyika Broadcasting Corporation, the Co-operative Union of Tanganyika Workers (NUTA), and Umoja wa Wanawake wa Tanganyika (UWT), should also be represented. Such an assemblage of men and women with varied interests but with a unity of purpose in nation-building would undoubtedly afford the Tanzania Library Association the desired opportunity to demonstrate its role as one of the agencies that is in a strategic position to assume leadership in the adult-education movement and to project the library's potential as an adult-education institution.

The 1970 Annual General Conference should initiate the formation of an Adult Education Library Service Division of the Tanzania Library Association. The establishment of this Division would offer librarians from all kinds of libraries the chance to get together to discuss and promote the educational services of libraries in general. The birth of an Adult Service Division in 1970 would reflect the determined effort of the Tanzania Library Association to bring about the recognition of the adult-education function of libraries. Thus, a sense of unity in the diversity of services would have been developed.

The role of the Tanzania Library Association in serving adult education may be classified in three general categories, namely, stimulating the participation of libraries in adult education, secondly, offering training activities for library staff in the role of libraries and librarians in adult education and, thirdly, developing co-operative relations with other agencies and organisations which have a concern for adult education.

The Association, through the Tanganyika Library Service and the Adult Education Library Service Division, could develop a comprehensive and up-to-date collection of books and pamphlets on adult-education principles and methods. The programme materials of other agencies and organisations are needed in order to understand their contributions to adult education. Exhibits of all the materials should be available for branch libraries to use as suggestions for building their own collections and for promoting their educational activities.

The Tanganyika Library Service and the Adult Services Division of the Association could begin to build up some special collections of films, especially in Swahili, and could make these available for adult-education programmes. Two examples of such films[28] are the new Kiswahili film on Tanzania entitled "Tanzania Yasonga Mbele" (Tanzania Forges Ahead), which is expected to be produced soon by the Korean Ministry of Culture. Secondly the "Metric Film", which is a ten-documentary film in Kiswahili and English, depicting the change from the imperial to the metric system of measurements in domestic, commercial and industrial circles in Tanzania, Kenya and Uganda. Audio-visual materials, including musical and non-musical recordings, filmstrips and radio, also serve the educational and cultural functions of libraries and should therefore be popularized. Instead of emphasizing the separateness of book and non-book materials, the concern should be with the content and the educational purposes of all materials of communication, in order to achieve the best learning situation. In other words, the end and not the means must be the determining factor.

The government has no plans to introduce television in the near future. Announcing this in Parliament on 16 June 1970, during question time, the Minister for Information and Tourism, Mr. Makame, told the National Assembly that it was not the intention of the government to introduce things from which only a few would benefit, because, if it did, it would go against the declared policies of the country. He added, however, that the government has decided to improve its radio services, because most people could afford a radio set.

In the first place, librarians could participate actively in many adult-education activities. Publicising the library's educational function in the pages of *Someni,* the quarterly journal of the Tanzania Library Association, and other periodicals is the standard procedure for many. Librarians who wish to extend their library's effectiveness as an educational institution will recognize the importance of making the library known to

---

[28] (*a*) The new Kiswahili film on Tanzania entitled "Tanzania Yasonga Mbele". Reviewed in the *Standard of Tanzania*. (*b*) The Metric Film. Reviewed in the *Nationalist* on 17 April 1970, p. 5, and in the *Standard of Tanzania* on 19 April 1970, p. 3.

others who are in organisations and agencies which are basically interested in working with adults. By joining and participating in these groups, librarians can increase the public's understanding of the library's potential role in adult education. Secondly, the Tanzania Library Association could offer and organise workshops and seminars for in-service training, with emphasis on adult-education knowledge and processes. In-service training workshops could cover the following topics: the adult-education role of the public library, community study, effectiveness of audio-visual aids in adult-education programming, selection and use of books for adults, and policies in selecting books for adults. Workshops, seminars and conferences have always been the principal methods of providing training and experience. They provide opportunities for wide co-operation and also the involvement of lay leaders from local communities.

The third major role of the Tanzania Library Association in serving adult education is that of developing co-operative relationships with other national agencies and organisations concerned with adult education. The Adult Education Association, the Institutes of Education and Swahili Research of the University, publishers and booksellers could co-operate with libraries in an effort to find out readers' interests and reading abilities, the different levels of materials to meet the varying abilities of adults, to define the qualities of readability and to compile lists of available books to meet these criteria. Book-reviewing and appraising, aimed at working out some means of grading books as to their suitability for different kinds of readers, would be the fruit of co-operation.

The Association could initiate projects such as a library community project in co-operation with other agencies to study and develop long-term adult-education programmes in selected areas based on an analysis of community need. Such a project, carried out through face-to-face interviews, questionnaires and demonstration libraries, when completed, could provide a broad basis of service and enable the national agencies to understand trends and possible needs for services.

Ujamaa villages, particularly Kabuku Ndani, Kabuku Barabarani, Segera and Horohoro, where adult-education campaigns are going on, the National Service Training Camps and Kivukoni College could form sample communities of special interest.

By developing friendly co-operative relationships with other national agencies and organisations, the Tanzania Library Association will reap many benefits for itself and for libraries all over the country. It will be able to promote the concept that libraries are educational institutions and that there are certain roles they may logically assume in the nation's adult-education programme.

Conclusion

There is no doubt that libraries and adult education in Tanzania have a very bright future. Adult education has proved to be one of the most promising innovations in the field of education in the development of the country. The literacy campaign has been intensified and literate adults are on the increase. Workers have accepted adult education as a challenge and are responding to the call of the leaders for self-improvement. The existing close relationship, based on mutual confidence and respect, between the adult-education agencies and the popular movements of the country should be maintained. As long as the adult educators maintain their basic sympathy for the aims and aspirations of the popular movements, including the political movement, and as long as the leaders trust tutors and adult students enough to allow free discussion of controversial issues, so long will adult education prosper and enable us to educate ourselves to the best of our abilities and to use our education for the benefit of all. President Nyerere has always emphasized the importance of free discussion and debate of government policies, in order to evoke constructive criticisms and to help the government leaders in planning future development programmes. The press and radio, which are the media for such discussion and debate, should, the President said, be fully used by all people who believe they have a point to make. Answering questions at the University College, the President challenged the third-year education students: "If intellectuals like you do not write, it is your fault: I cannot write for you."

And wishing them good luck in their careers, Mwalimu said: "Among other things, teach debate; but debate about socialism, not colonialism."[29]

The same goes for the libraries. The increased awareness of the importance of libraries, coupled with the general goodwill enjoyed by all the libraries, is a good omen. The existing high degree of library-mindedness among our leaders, including the President himself, augurs well for the present and future library development, which by implication means better library service to adult education in Tanzania.

As the future economic, political and social development of this country is inextricably bound up with the future of adult education, these omens give grounds for great optimism for the future. The policy and aims of adult education have been established upon sound and permanent foundations. The thriving present gives assurance that an even more prosperous future lies ahead. The leaders of this country are determined to turn the country into a nation of workers and peasants who are committed to educating themselves throughout their lives.

Selected bibliography

Christian Rural Fellowship of East Africa. Conference Report: 26–30 Sept., 1969, Moshi, Tanzania: Intermediate technology and integrated extension. (i) An integrated programme for adult education, pp. 24–25. (ii) The role of a community school in rural development, pp. 27–29.

Cowan, L. Gray, O'Connell, James, and Scanlon, D. G. (eds.). *Education and Nation-building in Africa.* London, Pall Mall Press, 1965, pp. 43–52 (Education in the Colonial Framework).

Coles, Edwin Townsend. *Adult Education in Developing Countries,* London, Pergamon Press, 1969.

[29] *The Nationalist of Tanzania,* 12 February 1970, p. 1: "Nyerere stresses discussion".

Dintenfass, Phyllis. *How to Adapt and Use Reading Materials: A Teacher's Guide*. Nairobi, Oxford Univ. Press, 1967.

Dodd, William A. *Education for Self-Reliance in Tanzania: A Study of Its Vocational Aspects*. New York, Teachers College Press, Columbia University; Center for Education in Africa, Institute of International Studies, 1969.

Fafunwa, A. Babs. *New Perspectives in African Education*. Lagos, Macmillan & Co., 1967, pp. 155-163 (Adult Education and National Service).

Nyerere, Julius K. *Non-alignment in the 1970s*. Opening address given on Monday, 13 April 1970, to the Preparatory Meeting of the Non-Aligned Countries, 13-17 April 1970. Dar-es-Salaam, The Government Printer, 1970, pp. 12.

Rweyemamu, A. H. (ed.). *Nation-building in Tanzania: Problems and Issues*. Nairobi, East African Publishing House, 1970, pp. 22-34.

Segal, S. S. *No Child Is Ineducable: Special Education—Provision and Trends*. Oxford, Pergamon Press, 1967, pp. 138-152.

Staffing. Teacher Education Institutions in East Africa: Supply and Demand, Training and Utilization. Report of the University of East Africa Conference on Teacher Education, 13-15 October 1969, pp. 10-19. Edited by Carl J. Manore. Dar-es-Salaam.

Strowbridge, Nancy (comp.). *Education in East Africa 1962-1968: A Selected Bibliography*. Makerere University College Library, 1969 (pp. 19-24, Tanzania). Makerere Library Publications No. 5.

Wilson, Louis Round. *Education and Libraries: Selected Papers*. Edited by Maurice F. Tauber and Jerrold Orne. Chapel Hill, The Shoe String Press, Inc., 1966, p. 67.

Education in Africa. Reprinted by the World Confederation of Organizations of the Teaching Profession from *Panorama*, Vol. 1, No. 4, 1959. Washington. WCOTP 1959, pp. 11-14; 28-30.

Field Report on the Survey of the Status of the Teaching Profession in Africa. In preparation for the World Confederation of Organizations of the Teaching Profession. Commission on Educational Policy for Africa (CEPA). Study of Recruitment and Retention of Teachers. Washington, WCOTP, 1967, pp. 108-111.

Parker, Franklin (comp.). *African Education: A Bibliography of 121 U.S.A. Doctoral Dissertations*. Washington. World Confederation of Organizations of the Teaching Profession 1965, pp. 42-44 (The Possible Role of Adult Education in Developing the Egyptian Rural Communities), Indiana University, 1958. 331 pp. Source: Diss. Abst. XIX, No. 5 (Nov. 1958), 1008-1009.

*Report of the East African Literary Training Seminar for Lead-

ers of Non-Governmental Organizations. Organized by the World Confederation of Organizations of the Teaching Profession on behalf of the NGO (Non-Governmental Organisations: UNESCO). Standing Committee in Collaboration with the UNESCO and its sub-regional Library Centre for East Africa and the Institute of Adult Education, University College, Dar-es-Salaam, held at the Nyegezi Social Training Centre, Mwanza, Tanzania. Washington, WCOTP, 1966, pp. 37–40.

P. J. Mhaiki

Libraries Are Assets in National Development

Many readers will remember their student days, when the school library was a fascination, a source of inspiration and a direct contributor to a successful school career. In many countries today, a home library is a status symbol, occupying a prominent place in the sitting-room.

The time has come now in Socialist Tanzania, where we believe in the dignity of man, in the equality of all men and in the right of all men to be educated, not to allow books to be status symbols for the privileged few only but to spread books and disseminate knowledge in the cities and in the rural areas for the development of all the citizens. A village library should be a source of inspiration to the rural people, just as a town library is for the town people.

In developing countries like Tanzania, the contribution of libraries to development can be witnessed daily in the cities. The libraries are usually crowded, the demand for longer hours of opening is pressing and the demand for books is great. Indeed, one of the privileges and advantages which the worker in Dar-es-Salaam, Tanga, Moshi, Mwanza and Arusha enjoys over his fellow worker in the rural areas is the library facilities. Through the use of these library facilities, workers qualify for better jobs, qualify for university entrance, gain scholarships and generally become better-informed people. It is believed that improvement in these areas makes for higher production and development.

In Tanzania, the Tanganyika Library Service, working within the Five-year Development Plan, has a national programme for establishing libraries. New libraries have been opened in several towns and plans exist to extend similar services to other towns. The demand for such library facilities out-runs the financial resources. Besides the Tanganyika Library Service, the government opens libraries in every secondary school and college of national education. The public in the vicinity of these schools are encouraged to use these libraries. In various places, libraries established by town councils, missions and organisations exist, either for public or for private use. Nevertheless the existing libraries fall short of meeting the actual demand in the towns of Tanzania.

In Tanzania, 90% of the population lives in the rural areas. Plenty of the right kind of literature is essential to supplement the national literacy and adult-education programme geared to development in the rural areas. Without follow-up reading material and, even more, libraries, the effort to make people functionally literate will be futile. In the national functional adult-education programmes, which we are trying to implement in Tanzania, the rural population must be supplied with posters, flash cards and literature, simply and appropriately written and organised as rural libraries on health, agriculture, better food, child care, crafts and home economics. To make people literate is only a means; the end is to train them to be intelligent and habitual readers. Pains must be taken and plans must be made to encourage people to read. It was wrongly assumed in the past that, once people were literate, they would continue to read, without having any books to read. It is a sad experience to see that once-literate people have become illiterate again.

The effort to establish rural libraries in Tanzania is a fresh venture beset with many problems. We are faced with the problem of population dispersion, but this is being taken care of by the TANU and the government by establishing *ujamaa* villages—a number-one priority in the Five-year Development Plan. *Ujamaa* villages, therefore, are our first targets for establishing rural libraries. In the meantime we try to establish centres in accordance with the settlement and movement patterns of the people. Thus the primary societies, trading points and leaders' houses are among the places where centres are being established. The next problem is that of transportation. The regions, districts, and divisions are so extensive that it is beyond our immediate ability to cover them adequately with the meagre transport resources that we have. We require a fleet of Landrovers for adult-education purposes, which could at the same time transport literature and book boxes into the rural areas. With the available funds, we are trying to provide at least one Landrover for each district to help to perform the many tasks of adult education. Our next problem is the availability of books in the national language, Swahili. At the present, it is estimated that there are about 500 titles in Swahili, which is the national language of two nations, Tanzania and Kenya, and which we hope will one day be the common language of East Africa. The potentialities of Swahili as a literary language in all respects are great. The need to develop Swahili and to write more books in it has never been felt more urgently than now. Funds must be found to write and print many books for adult education. The National Advisory Council on Adult Education, at a recent meeting, urged inter-ministerial co-operation in producing reading material for rural people. Our final problem is in the distribution of the written materials produced by various ministries. Many useful books, pamphlets, charts, magazines and newspapers end up in offices, instead of reaching the rural people. More often than not, this is caused by lack of regular transport facilities into the rural areas and to a small extent it is due to lack of organisation. Both these aspects need to be improved. It is surprising, though, to see that commercial articles, like Fanta and Sportsman cigarettes, reach the remotest areas, while reading materials do not. With better distribution arrangements, it should be possible to distribute books to the rural areas effectively.

The bigger the difficulties, the greater is the challenge and the greater is our determination to overcome these obstacles. The satisfaction derived from the achievements will be equal to the difficulties surmounted. There would be no point in planning and struggling if there were no difficulties.

We are advancing by planned stages in introducing libraries in the rural areas. The government is experimenting with a

Work-oriented Adult Literacy Project, with the assistance of the UNESCO, in the four Lake Regions of Tanzania. This is our testing-ground with respect to the establishment of these rural libraries. We follow up our literacy teaching with a rural newspaper of local interest, written in the limited vocabulary used in the functional primers and printed in special bold characters. Even this is not too easy to read for the first three or four months. The literacy teacher has sections of the rural newspaper and reads them aloud. This is to awaken the interest of the pupils in the paper and to make them aware of this instrument. As they gain confidence, the faster learners and abler students will lead the reading, which is followed by discussion and criticism. After six months, they can read this rural newspaper. While this is going on, we are making an effort, with the help of the Tanganyika Library Service, to establish a permanent library in the village for the use of the literates. To encourage the new literates to read, we ask a literate person to explain what he has read from *Ukulima wa Kisasa, Darubini* or *Kwetu* or from any interesting book. We ask one reader to actually read a chapter to a class and lead a discussion. This motivates the learners to learn faster, in order to be able to read these newspapers and books for themselves. Our greatest hope is that the discussion group will include literates of long standing, together with newly literate persons, so that they can exchange ideas, while at the same time those who are only just literate gain more confidence and feel the drive to utilize their newly acquired ability to read. *Contact* between the literate and the illiterate in the same environment is made possible through the use of the same village library.

We would also like to run commentaries on documentaries and factual films drawing information directly from the books, quoting the books and referring people to those books in their village library.

The opening of a village library is given maximum publicity. Government and Party leaders are usually invited to open the library and explain to the villagers the importance of libraries for the mental, social, economic and political development of the villagers. To our satisfaction, people read avidly and the problem is to supply sufficient books to satisfy the demand. This experiment is being now applied on a national basis.

It is not possible to establish a library in every village because of the lack of funds, books, suitable premises and personnel. We therefore also resort to the system of mobile libraries. Each District Adult-education Organiser is supplied with 500 books. He is supposed to put these on the Landrover and take them around the villages and schools which are adult-education centres and lend these books to the villagers. After some weeks this officer is supposed to visit these centres again to enable the villagers to change the books. We encourage our readers to hold discussion groups on the books read. If the facilities become available, we want to play to our rural people tape-recorded books and follow the readings with discussions. We have not yet done this.

Adult education is an old activity in Tanzania. Much political, health, agricultural and religious education has been carried out by oral communication. It has been successful in bringing about national unity and independence, but the oral method alone is no longer enough now. In a country like Tanzania, where transportation is difficult, where the leaders in all walks of life are very busy, and where the mass media are insufficiently developed, communication by the oral method cannot replace the printed word. For effective communication, in all aspects of development in the modern world, the ability to read and write is a necessary skill and is the foundation of development.

The habit of reading must be encouraged, cultivated and nursed. There should be a systematic approach to it and the more systematic the better. The extension officer, the politician and the preacher in Tanzania should look forward to the day when, after his address, he will be able to refer his audience to a book, a pamphlet, a magazine or a newspaper. A library in each village hall would be the ideal thing. Reading will stimulate mental activity, challenge parochial and traditional ideas, expand the scope of the readers' thinking, instil a desire in them to achieve, take them back into history to converse with the sages of many nations and project them into the exciting scientific future. Visits by important people will then be more educational and more time will be spent in dialogue, in discussing questions and problems with informed people.

A reading nation is a well-informed nation. It cannot be easily cheated or exploited. Education is a human right, and socialistic governments have the duty to exploit all possible means of educating their people. Libraries offer the opportunity to fulfil this obligation. Adult education of the right kind, supplemented with libraries, is a force for the intellectual, social, political and economic development of Tanzania. The development of this country will be brought about by an enlightened people released from the shackles of illiteracy and general ignorance. That is the goal of Tanzania.

T. K. Lwanga

The Library of Makerere University

University College at Makerere, just outside Kampala, the capital city of the Republic of Uganda, was founded in 1949 as a college for higher education affiliated to the University of London. With the establishment of the University of East Africa on 29 June 1963, the period of special relation with the University of London came to a close and degrees of the University of East Africa were instituted. The constituent Colleges of the University of East Africa were University College, Makerere, University College, Nairobi, and University College, Dar-es-Salaam.

Makerere University[1] is the oldest and largest institution of higher learning in East Africa. There are six faculties at Makerere: Agriculture, Arts, Education, Medicine, Science and Social Sciences. The University is also well known for its School of Fine Art, the East African School of Librarianship, the Makerere Institute of Social Research (formerly known as the East African Institute of Social Research), the Centre for Continuing Education (formerly the Department of Extra-Mural Studies), and the National Institute of Education. The University provides courses leading to about 37 awards of diplomas and degrees, including Ph.D.'s.

The total enrolment for the current academic year 1969–70 is about 2 500, including some 250 postgraduate degree and diploma students. The number of academic and senior administrative staff exceeds 300. The staff and students, and many

---

[1] Makerere University (formerly University College, Makerere) was established as a separate university on 1 July 1970.

scholars from other parts of the world, carry out vigorous research programmes. Thus the campus library clientele is quite complex. By its very nature, as the only important and large general library in Uganda, the University Library has to serve many people outside the University. The serious advanced student has nowhere else to turn but to the University Library. The same is true of public officers, teachers, doctors, librarians, etc., who are officially recognised by the University as people whom the University libraries have to serve. Through their photographic services and inter-library loans these libraries provide materials to researchers and scholars throughout East Africa.

This rather complex clientele is served by a system of four related libraries, consisting of the Main Library, the Medical Sub-library, the National Institute of Education Sub-library, and the Kabanyolo Farm Sub-library, together with the autonomous Makerere Institute of Social Research Library and a number of departmental libraries.

Established senior professional staff, 1966-1970

1966–67	1967–68	1968–69	1969–70

Main Library (including the Librarian and Deputy Librarian)

6	8	9	9

Medical Library (Albert Cook Library)

1	1	1	1

National Institute of Education (Sub-library)

1	1	1	1

Senior professional staff here means university graduates who are also qualified librarians. There are four Ugandans and seven expatriates.

In addition to the 11 university graduate librarians, the University libraries are manned by nine non-graduate librarians, (and university graduates without professional training) and well over 50 non-professional staff.

Status

The senior professional staff have academic status in the University. The Librarian is equated with a professor; the Deputy Librarian has Senior Lecturer rank, and the rest of the senior staff are graded as Lecturers.

The Library is rated as a department. However, with the rapid expansion in all fields, it may not be very long before it will be accorded faculty status.

Training

In 1967 the College (as it was then) embarked on a phased programme of training for Ugandans to fill the senior professional posts. By the end of the 1968–69 academic year six graduates had been recruited and sent to Britain to take postgraduate courses in librarianship. The intermediate supporting staff are trained locally at the East African School of Librarianship.

Finance, 1966-1970

Expenditure on books and periodicals (including binding costs) for all the library services is estimated as follows (in pounds sterling):

	1966–67	1967–68	1968–69	1969–70
Main Library	13 525	20 500	27 550	26 000
Albert Cook Library	3 345	4 500	4 800	5 800
Kabanyolo Library	—	—	300	500

For the Main Library, the figure for 1968–69 of £27 550 includes additional funds of £6 500 received by way of supplementary budget. For 1967–70, £5 000 per year were earmarked for capital expenditure on back runs of periodicals required to fill existing gaps in our collection.

Library Committee

The Main College Library Committee is a standing committee of the Academic Board. Its duty is, in consultation with the Librarian, to make recommendations to the Academic Board on general library policy.

The Committee was re-constituted in 1967 to make it stronger and to make faculties, departments and the student body better informed of library policies. The membership of the Committee is as follows: the Principal; three members elected by the Academic Board, of whom at least two should be members of the Academic Board; seven elected members, one from each Faculty; two representatives of the Students' Guild; the Librarian; and the Deputy Librarian, as Secretary of the Committee.

Sub-committees

There are sub-committees for the sub-libraries, and these report to the Main College Library Committee. These sub-committees are responsible for formulating the general policies of their sub-libraries. They deal with such matters as opening hours, rules and regulations for the use of the library, and the selection of new acquisitions. The Librarian is a member of the sub-committees.

Acquisitions procedures

For the Main College Library, the annual vote is divided up into departmental votes, excluding departments served by the sub-libraries. A large sum is also left unallocated and this is spent at the discretion of the Librarian. The expenditure of the departmental library votes is the responsibility of each Head of Department. He has to make regular recommendations to the Librarian of new books and periodicals to be purchased from his department's library allocation. The procedure has the advantage of directly involving the teaching staff in book selection. It leaves the Librarian the main task of selecting materials which bridge gaps between subjects and the supplementary material which must be in any good university library. In essence, the Librarian is in overall charge of the acquisitions, working with—as it were—a committee composed of the Heads of Departments.

As already mentioned above, the acquisitions of the sub-libraries are selected by the sub-committees, who consider recommendations from the teaching staff and the sub-librarian.

The Main College Library

The Main Library building has been described by a former Makerere Deputy Librarian as "a jewel of modern tropical architecture, set centrally in a campus noted for its beauty. With floor-to-ceiling windows all round, it is light and airy. An arrangement of individual study tables placed one behind the other in a row next to the windows, with open book and periodical stacks on the inside, creates an atmosphere conducive to study and quiet" (*College and Research Libraries,* Vol. 29, No. 3, p. 201). This is all very true, and you can immediately tell that the gentleman fell deeply in love with the Makerere Library. But it is also true that the College Main Library is in a way a good example of the fact that one can never plan a library which is too large. The original part of the present building was completed in 1958, but soon, in a space of just two years, it was felt necessary to have it extended. In 1962 an extension of about one-third of the present building was added. We have now, already, in a span of six years, embarked on yet another extension, slightly larger than the existing building (50 000 sq. ft. floor area).

The Main College Library is the most important general research library in East Africa. It is the Legal Deposit Library for Uganda, under the Deposit Library Act of 1958. It has a collection of some 125 000 accessioned volumes of books and pamphlets, 40 000 government documents and publications of international organisations, and some 150 000 volumes of back issues of periodicals. Some 2 250 periodicals are received regularly. Annual accessions are about 9 000 books.

In addition to the traditional orders and cataloguing sections, the Main Library consists of a periodicals section, a circulation/reference section, a bindery, a printing press (which is in the process of becoming a separate unit as the University Press), and a photographic-services section. There is also a special-collections section, which is one of the most important features of the Library.

The special collections are kept in a separate enclosed section of the Library, which is administered by an Assistant Librarian. It has a seating capacity of 25 readers and five research tables. Because of the nature of the material, the size of the room and the circulation space available, the collections are not accessible without permission. The special collections include:

1. *Africana (books and periodicals)*. This collection consists of:

(a) All publications relating to East Africa, i.e. Kenya, Tanzania and Uganda. The East Africana form the main bulk of the collection.

(b) All really old or valuable Africana, and the publications one would expect to find in any good Africana collection.

(c) All the older books by explorers, travellers, hunters, etc., which are of little use on the open shelves but are fascinating to Africanists.

(d) All publications in African languages.

(e) All publications on Africa, the political interest of which renders them liable to be stolen, if placed on the open shelves.

(f) Publications on countries bordering East Africa, where their subject matter seems to warrant it. However, materials on Somalia, Ethiopia, Malawi, Ruanda and Burundi are not counted as East Africana, except in the latter two cases, as these territories were part of German East Africa.

The current acquisition policy is to acquire copies of all publications of and about East Africa. General materials on Africa as a whole or on a specific African country or area go on the open shelves.

2. *Official documents*. These form the largest part of the special collections. They comprise the following two categories:

(a) *Government publications*. Here the aim is only to have a complete collection of the publications of the East African Community and the official documents of the East African countries (Kenya, Tanzania and Uganda). In the case of Uganda, one copy of all official publications is received automatically as a *legal deposit*. With regard to the East African Community, Kenya and Tanzania, there is an uncertain long-standing agreement that one free copy of all their publications should automatically be sent to us. The acquisition of official publications of all other countries is selective. For example, Norway sends only its statistical yearbook, whereas from Zambia we receive nearly everything.

(b) *United Nations and international organizations publications*. Since 1958 the Library has been a U.N. deposit library. Therefore we receive all the printed publications of the U.N. and its agencies. We also receive free copies of most of the publications of other international organisations.

3. *Microcards and microfilms*. The Library has a number of items in this form. These include newspapers, theses, archives, periodicals, etc.

4. *Archives and manuscripts*. The archives and manuscripts are kept together. These are almost all private collections which have been handed over to the Library under varying prescribed conditions of use. They include some of the very valuable collections, such as the following:

Bageshawe, A. G. Diaries (manuscript: 5 vols.).
Baskerville, George K. Journals 1890–1901 (manuscript: 7 vols.).
Church Missionary Society. Papers of the Upper Nile Mission 1926–1948 (manuscript: 7 vols.).
Jacobs, B. L. Papers (official) etc. *c.* 1960 (typescript and manuscript: 7 boxes) (including Uganda Independence Celebration office files).
Kabali, Ezera. Papers, 1900 onwards (manuscript and typescript: 8 boxes, 1 vol.).
Kagwa Family. (Mengo, Buganda) Papers. Various dates 1899–1947 (manuscript: 52 boxes).
Kivebulaya, Apolo. Material concerning Apolo Kivebulaya (manuscript, etc.: 1 box) (includes his diaries and photographs etc. concerning him, forming the basis of Anne Luck's *African Saint*).
Ladbury, H. Boulton. Journal of missionary work in Uganda 1903–1950 (manuscript: 5 vols.).
Maine, Sir Amar. Papers. *c.* 1946–.
Miti, James. Notebooks etc. for History of Buganda. *c.* 1940.
Native Anglican Church (Uganda). Archives of the Archbishop's

office. 1900 onwards (manuscript) (including minute books, ledgers, journals, miscellaneous correspondence, etc.) (16 boxes).

Native Anglican Church (Uganda). Educational administration. Archives. Various dates 1930– (manuscript and typescript) (consists of files of minutes of local education committees and papers concerning Education Commission) (29 bundles of files, 1 vol., 1 box).

The Albert Cook (Medical) Library holds the early casebooks and papers of the Mengo Hospital.

5. *University collection.* This consists of the following material:

(*a*) Theses and dissertations by members of the staff of the University.

(*b*) *College and University archives.* All material emanating from or about the College and the University. When a work can equally or preferably be placed in the East African collection, it is placed there. This material is kept separately in filing cabinets.

6. *Photographic collection.* This collection is almost entirely made up of photographs deposited, on permanent loan to the Library, by the late Dr. Schofield. They contain some of the rare photographs of events and scenes of Uganda history.

The Albert Cook Library (Medical Library)

The Albert Cook Library, which is a branch of the University Library, is situated in the Medical School on Mulago Hill. It is named after Sir Albert Cook, the C.M.S. missionary, who came to Uganda in February 1897 and founded the C.M.S. Hospital at Mengo. One of the Library's most prized collections is that of the personal notebooks of Sir Albert Cook, together with the Mengo case notes dating from 1897, meticulously recorded in his own handwriting, and the files of his letters, which provide a valuable historical record of the early days of the development of medicine in Uganda.

The first Medical School collection consisted mainly of textbooks and monographs and a few tattered journals. With the fusion in 1946 of this collection with the Mengo Hospital collection, consisting mainly of the notebooks of Sir Albert Cook, the first Medical Library came into being. The total collection comprised 5 000 volumes. The collection grew rapidly over the next 10 years as a result of many generous gifts from various medical schools. By June 1959, when the Library moved into its present building, the stock had increased to 15 000 volumes.

The new Library was a two-storey rectangular building measuring 85′ × 42′ (approx. 7 200 sq. ft.), constructed across the slope of the hill. The design was based upon a multiplication of units or "modules" of 17′ × 14′ (approx. 240 sq. ft.), with the idea of later extending it by the addition of similar "modules" at one end. It had accommodation for 36 000 volumes and could seat 60 readers.

The proposal in the University Development Plan to increase the intake of students to 90 in July 1965 demanded an extension to the Library. The extension, together with the old block, was calculated to provide seats for a third of the potential reading capacity of 500 (i.e. 160 seats) and an additional shelf space of 14 000 volumes, making a total shelf capacity of 50 000 volumes for the next 15 years' growth.

The extended Library, completed in 1966, is nearly double its original size, as is shown by the following figures:

	Old Library	Extension	New Library
Floor area (sq. ft.)	7 200	4 560	11 760
Seats	60	100	160
Shelving (vols.)	36 000	14 000	50 000

The Albert Cook Library is the largest collection of medical literature in East Africa and compares favourably with many of the large medical libraries overseas. It now has nearly 30 000 accessioned volumes of books and periodicals and receives regularly some 500 current periodicals. It serves the staff and students of the Medical School, the staff of Mulago Hospital and doctors and research workers throughout East Africa.

Makerere Institute of Social Research Library

This Library is primarily a small centre for research in the social sciences—economics, political science, rural economy, and sociology. It has some 4 000 books, together with a substantial collection of dissertations, conference papers, pamphlets, government publications, unpublished manuscripts, and about 80 periodicals. The Institute carries out one of the most vigorous research programmes of the University.

Use of the Library is limited to members only. These include staff and post-graduate students of the relevant departments, fellows and associates, and individual members of the Institute who come from outside the University.

As from 1970, the Library will no longer be autonomous, but will become a sub-library of the Main College Library and will be manned by a qualified librarian.

Expenditure on books and periodicals is estimated at about £1 000 per annum. A good deal of material is acquired as donations, and through exchange arrangements.

The National Institute of Education Sub-library

The library at the Institute of Education was established as a separate unit in 1962. Until 1965 it remained completely autonomous.

In that year it was brought into a relationship with the Main Library similar to that of the Medical Sub-library. However, the connection is not identical, owing to its different constitution and financial support. A library committee with members from the Institute and the University, including the Librarian, decides policy matters and a sub-committee considers book and periodical purchases.

The Sub-library serves the Faculty of Education and the students for its Bachelor of Education degree and post-graduate Diploma in Education, as well as the Institute of Education, which conducts up-grading courses for tutors in the Uganda teacher-training colleges. The staff of schools and training colleges throughout Uganda also use the Sub-library.

Postal loans and photocopying services are available to teacher-training colleges.

The total stock of the Sub-library is now about 20 000 books, pamphlets, reports, and theses. Some 150 periodical titles are received annually.

Kabanyolo Farm Sub-library

The University Farm is situated about 10 miles from the main campus. About 80 second-year agriculture students spend a full academic year at the Farm, plus six weeks during vacations. There are also over 20 post-graduate students doing research work at the Farm. Because of the distance and the numbers of students and staff involved, it was found necessary in 1968 to provide a small specialised library service at the Farm. We are still in the process of building up a good representative stock of books and periodicals covering the various subjects taught at the Farm.

The wider role and status of the University Library

We believe, at Makerere, that the role of the University Library should be clearly seen and recognised to be that of a national reference and research library. This, I am sure, is also the view held by the majority of leading librarians in East Africa and in many other developing countries, that this is the role the university library should play in the development of library services.

In Uganda, we visualise three main streams of development of library services; the public library, serving the general population in cities, towns and rural areas; special libraries, including government departmental and research libraries; and college libraries and the University Library, the latter acting also as the national reference library with a wide range of research collections.

There are sound reasons for this kind of thinking and planning, both in terms of finance, professional staff, and availability of rare material. We find that, inevitably, much of the material necessary for all aspects of research (which should be in a national reference collection) is basic also to university research needs; also the academic core of the country is largely to be found centred upon the University.

As already mentioned above, by virtue of the Makerere University College (Depository Library) Act of 1958, the Library became a legal depository for Uganda publications. It is also a depository in Uganda for the publications of major international organisations, such as the United Nations Organisation, the World Health Organisation, the International Labour Office and the Food and Agriculture Organisation. The Library has established wide exchange arrangements with well over 1 000 learned institutions throughout the world. The Main Library has built up over the years a large and unique East African collection. Thus, by the very nature of its content and organisation and in the absence of a well-developed public-library service or national library, the Makerere Library finds itself obliged to assume the responsibilities of a national reference library.

What do we mean by a national reference library? We mean not only a library which collects material published within the country and material about the country published elsewhere, but also a library in which there is a large concentration of research materials covering a wide range of subjects. Its collections are at once both extensive and intensive in their subject coverage. They are not intended to be a substitute for research, government or public libraries, but rather a comprehensive collection that will supplement these libraries when their requirements go beyond normal needs.

Plans for the official recognition of the Makerere Library as the national reference library have been put to the government for legislation. Once this role is granted, then the logical consequence of the Library's operation will be for it also to be designated as the centre for the international exchange of official publications. The exchange programme would enable the Library to send official publications to other overseas institutions, particularly universities, and in turn the Library would receive material issued by them. This systematic exchange arrangement would enrich the Library's holdings.

We also feel that the status of a national reference library should include the right to microfilm and distribute film copies as exchange media.

The Makerere Library will, of course, have to brace itself to meet the commitments which the new status will bring with it. The following are only a few of them:

(a) *Book-stock expansion.* Inevitably some additional financial provision will have to be made for material not normally acquired for the University.

(b) *Shelving and reading space.* The accelerated rate of acquisition, and the expected increase in donations and deposits will most definitely require more shelving space. The Library will also have to shoulder increased responsibility for opening its doors to accredited non-university readers; hence the need for more well-planned reading space.

(c) *Additional staff.* We recognise that more staff on all levels will be required. Already the University has embarked on a phased scheme of recruiting university graduates for training in librarianship, and a vigorous training programme is also in force for the intermediate grades of staff.

(d) *National bibliographical centre.* The Library, as the national reference library, will have to be responsible for producing a national bibliography. There is, at the moment, no institution in Uganda—let alone East Africa—which produces a comprehensive national bibliography.

We at Makerere have already recognised the great need in this field. An attempt at compiling a Uganda Bibliography was started at the beginning of 1965. A "Uganda Bibliography" section appeared for the first time in the Makerere University College Library Bulletin and Accessions List, No. 55, January–February 1965. The Bibliography includes material (including government publications) received on legal deposit and books, etc. about Uganda published outside the country.

These then are the general development and the future plans for library services at Makerere University.

The University Library, Nairobi

McMillan Memorial Library, Nairobi

The Campus of the University of Dar es Salaam

The Headquarters of the Tanganyika Library Service, Dar es Salaam

Makerere University Library, Kampala

Kampala Library

C. Kigongo-Bukenya

The Public Libraries Board in Uganda[1]

The Public Libraries Board is a body corporate and of perpetual succession established in 1964 and charged with establishing, equipping, managing and maintaining public libraries in Uganda.

Uganda was a British Protectorate and achieved independence in 1962. It is an equatorial country in East Africa bordered by the Sudan to the north, the Congo to the west and Rwanda, Tanzania and Lake Victoria to the south. The climate is tropical, with an average temperature of 71° Fahrenheit. The total area is 91 134 square miles, including 16 386 square miles of swamp and water.

For administrative purposes, Uganda is divided into four regions:

(a) The Eastern Region, comprising the districts of Bugisu, Bukedi, Busoga, Mbale municipality, Sebei and Teso.

(b) The Western Region, comprising the districts of Bunyoro, Toro, Ankole and Kigezi.

(c) The Buganda Region, with the islands in Lake Victoria, comprising the districts of Mengo, Masaka and Mubende, and

(d) The Northern Region, comprising the districts of Karamoja, Lango, Acholi, and West Nile.

The population is 9 526 000, including 9 000 Europeans and 88 000 Asians. The official language is English, but many Ugandans read and understand only their vernacular languages, of which there are many. Thirteen of them are impor-

[1] The views expressed in this article are those of the author and not those of the Board.

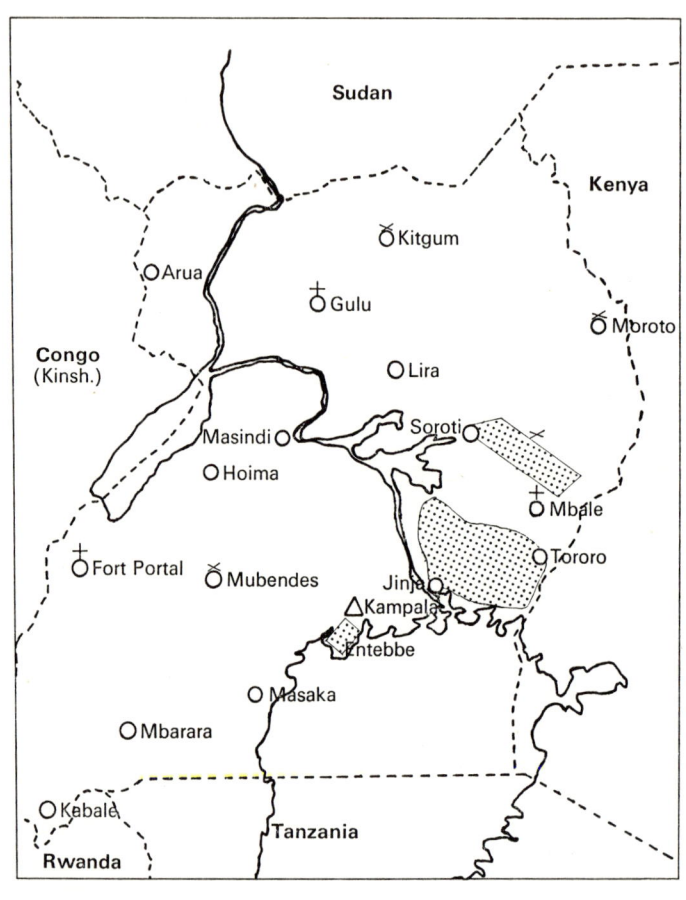

Uganda Library Service Points

O Existing Branch
☧ Regional Headquarters (proposed)
▨ Mobile Service
△ Central Headquarters
× Closed

tant and Luganda is the most widely used. Lake, marine, railway and some road services are operated by the East African Railways and Harbours Administration.

Education is a joint undertaking by the government, local authorities and to some extent voluntary agencies. The education system is divided into three sectors—primary, secondary and post-secondary. Further education is provided at the Uganda College of Commerce and the agricultural colleges. There are also several departmental training schools for training staff for different departments. University-level education is available at Makerere University in Kampala.

About a third of the population is literate. An adult literacy campaign directed towards the eradication of illiteracy was started in 1964. Under the Second Five-year Development Plan it is intended to give reading lessons to 200 000 people per year.

The monetary income *per capita* (at 1964 prices) is £25. The Second Five-year Development Plan envisages a rise to £50 by 1981.

Scope of the Public Libraries Board

The UNESCO Public Library Manifesto (1949) described the public library as "... a democratic institution operated by the people for the people ...: established and maintained under clear authority of law; supported wholly or mainly from public funds; open for free use on equal terms to all members of the community, regardless of occupation, creed, class or race ...".

The definition of the public library in Uganda does not differ from the above. A public library is any library:

(1) Established and maintained under the clear authority of the Public Libraries Act of 1964.

(2) Run mainly from the public funds (public funds here meaning money from the Uganda Treasury).

(3) Stocking library materials expressing all opinions, without bias or prejudice of any kind.

(4) Free for use by all Ugandans and by such people as are eligible, regardless of age, profession, class, creed or race.

In accordance with the definition, the University Library, catering for the academic community, the specialist libraries with their limitation to specialist clienteles, and the High Commission and Embassy libraries, stocking books published in and about their respective countries, do not come under the Public Libraries Board.

History of the Public Libraries Board

The origin of the Public Libraries Board stretches as far back as 1944, when the East African Governors commissioned Mrs. Elspeth Huxley to tour East Africa and recommend what the East African Governments should do to improve the provision of books and magazines for the African reading public. Her report, published in 1945, recommended setting up the East African Literature Bureau, which, among other responsibilities, would publish books in the vernacular languages of East Africa and provide a public lending-library service. C. D. Richard looked further into the problem and recommended the appointment of a public librarian to plan and administer the library service. This appointment was given to Mr. George Annesley, who investigated the factors to be considered in evolving a library service. The year 1948 saw two important happenings that were relevant to the development of the Public Libraries Board. It was during that year that the British Council established its offices in Nairobi and accepted the responsibility for inaugurating library services in East Africa, with a view to handing them over to the individual countries in running order. The same year saw the starting of the East Africa Literature Bureau, which, under the East African Libraries, was to provide a public-library service.

Meanwhile, in 1949 Mr. G. Annesley's scheme of library development was submitted to the East African Governments and to the Colonial Office. The scheme was approved in 1950, but, due to the expense involved, the scheme was restricted to the branches, leaving the headquarters as originally proposed.

At the time, each East African country had a committee for administering library affairs. All these committees unanimously agreed in 1959 to appoint a library-development adviser, who was to be entrusted with the duty of working with the library committees on long-term plans and was also to stay behind to put them into effect. Mr. S. W. Hockey was given the appointment. His report was ready by 1960 and it outlined the basic principles on which the East African countries were to found their public-library services. The principles included the setting up of a strong central library, emphasis on a children's library service, a generous staff-training scheme and a Library Act setting up the service.

Developments since the Library Act

The year 1964 can therefore be regarded as the turning-point in the development of the Public Libraries Board. It was then that the Uganda Parliament enacted the Library Act, thereby setting up a body corporate and of perpetual succession to provide the service. The Act ensured the permanency of the service, adequate financial support and efficient administration according to a national standard. It defined the functions of the Board and created the conditions under which it might fulfil those functions and ensure development.

The Minister of Culture and Community Development, using the powers given to him in the Act, announced the appointment of the Public Libraries Board on 10 November 1964. Nine members were appointed; four regional representatives, one city-council representative and four others. The chairman was the then Chief Education Officer, later the Director of the Centre of Continuing Studies and now Secretary to the Council of Makerere University. The vice-chairman was the principal of a teacher-training college and is now Chaplain of Makerere University. The other three members were Members of Parliament, while the rest were outstanding personalities in their respective circles.

Now that the Board was in existence, the next stage was the handing over of the services to it. The services up to that time were being managed by the Ministry of Culture and Community Development. The services included 11 branch libraries, a postal library service and a book-box service. Branches had been opened in gazetted towns, where demand was evident. The book-box service organised from Kampala was meant for depository centres, which were mostly schools, clubs and institutions. The postal library was also run from headquarters and was meant for those people in remote areas who lacked access to branch libraries.

After its inception and the handing over of the services to it, the Board started business. It held eight meetings during its first year of office (1965). At these meetings the Board discussed and drafted the terms of service for its employees, paying special regard to:

(*a*) Salaries, which it fortunately made generous enough to attract and retain men and women of the right calibre in the service.

(*b*) Granting of pensions, gratuities or retiring allowances to employees and requiring them to contribute to any pension, provident fund or superannuation scheme.

(*c*) Providing annual leave and leaves of absence for studies, etc.

(*d*) Regulations governing the staff, in order to foster understanding, good working relationships and efficiency, besides ensuring mobility of staff throughout Uganda.

The Board also tried to find out the basic and general principles on which to build the library service.

The Board was at the outset concerned with the question of staff, as regarded both quality and quantity. The Board had inherited about 40 members of staff who had been employees of the Bureau's libraries. These included three Assistant Librarians—previously qualified and trained teachers with reasonable library experience acquired in the service, coupled with a "workshop type of course" which provided them with the elementary principles of librarianship. There were two Senior Library Assistants, their seniority accruing from their long service and on-the-job experience. Next to these were 20 Library Assistants, recruited from varied walks of life, with the Cambridge Certificate or its equivalent.

There was the question of appointing the Director of the Services. The words of Edward Sydney can be quoted here:[1]

> The Ghana experience illustrates another principle which requires to be stated without equivocation. The establishment, organisation and early development of national library services in newly independent countries demand not only a high degree of professional, theoretical knowledge, but also much practical experience in the management of a large organisation and control ... of personnel, experience in the consideration and presentation of policies and considerable skill in the day-to-day administration of routine processes. It would seem wise therefore at the outset to buy these qualities wherever they can be got. No doubt the key appointment in any Public Library Service is that of the Chief Librarian (Director). Upon his knowledge and experience, upon his warmth of personality and upon his knack of getting on with people almost everything depends.

The Board appointed the only qualified librarian in the service as the first Director of the Service. True, the newly appointed Director had a sound education, technical qualifications and a reasonably long experience. He was a hard-working fellow too. But history records him as a man lacking administrative tact and the sense of good public relations within and without the service; indeed with a "let me go alone" attitude. These qualities brought the Board slow progress and a great deal of criticism.

The Director had started well by making a survey of Uganda to find out the actual state of the libraries. His findings that Uganda needed libraries to help with the social, political and economic development were correct. Indeed, the way he had envisaged the National Library Service plan in the short and long terms was a move in the right direction—the former to meet the country's immediate needs, which included supplementing the literacy campaign by providing suitable material

---

[1] Sydney Edward: Introduction to *Tropical Library Service* by Evelyn Evans, page xiv.

for the literates to practise their literacy on, and the latter to enable Uganda to develop a library service of its own, the goals being the preservation of published literature and the enabling of Ugandans to apply in their everyday life the record of what is known, thereby assisting them to contribute to their respective trades and professions.

However, the actual developments made were totally against the acknowledged principles of a library service. Instead of starting by founding and consolidating the central library (headquarters), to enable technical processes, administration of the service, extension activities and training of staff to be carried on there, he instead opened more branches and a mobile service. The principle behind this move—to provide library services to as many people as possible—was correct. However, it should have occurred to the Director, and he should have advised the Board, that, in inheriting the services that they had inherited, they had taken on far greater responsibility than the present resources, both of finance and personnel, could maintain. The wise step, therefore, would have been to postpone any expansion of the service and instead to concentrate on the headquarters and a few libraries. Expansion would take place only when resources were available. This was the move recommended by the Hockey Report, which Ghana found a necessity and the only way out in the case of inadequate staff. The development of the Tanzanian Library Service had gone far to remove any doubts about it.

While some efforts were made to build up the headquarters, they were all costly failures, since no proper personnel to man it were secured. The most disappointing failure was the omission of a generous training scheme for producing personnel to man and administer the service.

These were, therefore, two difficult years for the Public Libraries Board. The Board faced strong and bitter criticisms from the public and it had to act drastically to retrieve and maintain its name and public confidence. This it did by terminating the services of its first Director in November 1966. As will be seen, this was the end of one era and the beginning of another.

As it was, the Board had almost to start afresh. Naturally

takes made in the past. First priority has rightly been given to the founding of the headquarters on a firm basis to take up the following duties.

(1) Selection, purchase, processing, cataloguing and classification of book stock.

(2) The compilation and maintenance of the Union Catalogue to cut down duplication and at the same time to make resources available throughout the service.

(3) To provide a reference and information service, since the stock and staff are concentrated at headquarters.

The Processing Department—comprising two sections, the Selection and Acquisition Section and the Cataloguing Section—has made good progress. Selection and acquisition are now being supervised by qualified and trained personnel. Classification and cataloguing are performed by three qualified persons, who at the same time share the responsibility of compiling and maintaining the Union Catalogue and the Shelf List.

The Circulation Department is also making good progress. This includes the postal service, book-box service, mobile libraries, statistics, quarterly reports and inter-library loans.

The postal service serves the remote readers who have no access to either static libraries, the mobile libraries or the book-box services. The membership fee is 20 shillings; 10 shillings deposit, which is refundable on termination of membership, and a further sum of 10 shillings which is non-refundable and is used in respect of postage. Membership is declining, as more former members gain access to other service points. This service, however, still presents problems. It is not easy to furnish readers with up-to-date information concerning stock, many books get lost during transit and readers spend irritating periods without books to read, since there is a time lag between the sending of the request, its despatch and its reaching the reader.

The book-box service provides services to interested bodies, such as institutes, schools and colleges. Membership, which to-day totals 57 bodies spread all over the country, is 100 shillings per year per box. The boxes, each containing 100–200 books, can be retained for a maximum of six months, but books can be exchanged as often as need arises.

There are two mobile libraries serving areas of great existing and potential readership in the preparation of branch libraries. One operates in the Eastern Region in the districts of Busoga and Bukedi on a three-monthly basis and the other operates at Entebbe on a weekly basis. There has been a great response to these services; however, the cost of running them, especially that in the Eastern Region, is proving unbearable.

The Circulation Department, as the above description shows, is responsible for the actual distribution of stock to recipients wherever they are in Uganda. This Department is also supervised by qualified and trained personnel.

The Periodicals Department has also shown development. It is charged with the responsibility of acquiring periodicals (it now receives over 100 periodicals), processing them in conjunction with the Cataloguing Section, and storing them. It also caters for the East Africana collection—materials on East Africa and rare materials. This stock is meant for reference only.

Great attention is paid to the 17 branch libraries opened in the gazetted towns of Uganda, to ensure good and co-ordinated development. The biggest branches, Fort Portal and Mbale, are run jointly by the Public Libraries Board, the British Council and the local authorities. The Public Libraries Board provides senior staff and undertakes staff training, while the British Council provides funds for stock, premises, etc. Local authorities are gradually coming into the scheme by providing supporting staff. A few of the most active local authorities have set aside funds for area library buildings. Regular visits of inspection are made by the Acting Director or senior staff. Systematic checks on the running of the libraries are made during such visits and discussions with the branch staff are held, resulting in fruitful suggestions.

The training of staff has not been pushed into the background. At the time of writing, three members of staff have been awarded the Diploma in Librarianship (E.A.), after successfully passing all the parts of their final examinations. Two more have returned from the School of Librarianship at Makerere, after passing the first part of their final examination, and are now writing their individual papers, on which will depend the award of their Diploma in Librarianship (E.A.). In addition, six members of staff are attending library studies in the United Kingdom. The service now has 10 Senior Library Assistants, who have attended a course in library studies leading to the award of a Certificate in Library Studies. We also have the services of three expatriate librarians. At the present there is a continuous staff-training scheme to ensure that adequate staff are available to administer the service as it expands.

This is the position at present and the Board can now look forward with confidence and plan for the future. However, it is moving very cautiously and must justify whatever steps are to be taken.

The future

It is in the future that the present position will be consolidated. However, there are new projects in the pipeline. There is the Public Libraries Board headquarters building, with its pressing need for ample space for the housing of library materials as well as offices for the administration. A site for the headquarters has been secured in the centre of the city and the plans to get the necessary funds are under way.

A few local authorities, like Jinja and Soroti, are contemplating building functional library buildings for their branches and the Public Libraries Board has given them advice regarding the requirements for these buildings. The proposal still stands for building the three regional headquarters at Mbale, Gulu and Fort Portal for the Eastern, Northern and Western Regions respectively, in the hope of achieving decentralisation of the services. Negotiations for the materialisation of this proposal are being carried on.

The demand for library services is growing every day in Kampala and the present facilities at the Kampala Library are inadequate. It is therefore proposed that a mobile service for the area should be started.

Of late, concern has been expressed that the public library service is concentrated on urban areas. In future it is proposed to consolidate and expand the service to the rural areas. This means that more facilities will be available to the rural areas through the book-box, mobile-library and postal services. A community-centres book-box scheme is envisaged to cope with the demand that has naturally emanated from the literacy campaign.

The importance of the service to children is fully recognised. It is with this in mind that the Public Libraries Board is considering the improvement of the present provisions at the branches and through the mobile library. The Board realises that the most effective way of providing the children's service would be through a generous and comprehensive schools library service, which would of necessity involve the training of teachers so that they can assist in the scheme. There is much groundwork to be done before this service materialises, because the Ministry which oversees the Public Libraries Service is different from the Ministry of Education, which has the responsibility for the schools. The relationship between the two ministries has therefore to be defined before the service can be started. The Board is currently engaged on this problem.

Conclusion

In view of the present developments, the achievements and the nature and variety of the developmental plans envisaged, it is justifiable to conclude by suggestions which will further and help the achievement of the Public Libraries Board's cherished goals.

The Board will certainly have to talk more about libraries than it has ever done before, so that the government becomes more involved and the people more interested in the library service, to the point of extending their sympathies to its promotion and maintenance. It is on the government's belief and interest in a social service such as this that the service's growth depends. The government finances the service and (in circumstances like ours, in which we still depend on expatriates) it has to approve the recruitment of expatriates, not to mention the Board's arrangements for any kind of aid.

The government is therefore the arbiter of the service's destiny; once it is convinced of the need of the library services, the rest should be easy.

The Uganda Government has shown great interest in library development. It has provided funds, though they have been inadequate, as is the case all over the world, and has talked of its great plans regarding library services. Recently, when Professor W. L. Saunders, the Director of the Post-graduate School of Librarianship at the University of Sheffield, addressed the East African Library Association (Uganda Branch), the Commissioner for Community Development read the Minister's speech, in which he said: "Everything possible should be done to see that libraries spread to the furthest corners of Uganda and that every citizen will be able to borrow near his home."[1] In addition, the speech revealed that the Ministry of Regional Administration (the ministry governing the local authorities) had agreed to share the burden by providing land and buildings for libraries in urban areas.

More staff will have to be found to man the service points as well as to administer the service. This will guarantee efficiency and will show the serious intention of the Public Libraries Board to provide the service. Then, it is hoped, aid will be forthcoming from interested bodies and other countries. For indeed, what Mr. Broome, the Director of the Tanganyika Library Service, said is still true:

Every country which gives financial aid/assistance has a right to decide whether the money is going to be well spent; whether it is going to benefit the country in the way it is intended. It is therefore important not only to present worth-while schemes for consideration but to show that there are staff to implement the schemes when the money arrives.[2]

The Board must go all out to secure more funds for library development. Without adequate funds, development will slow down. In connection with this, W. Caldwell's words can be quoted: "... in these days of national financial stringency in

---

[1] *Uganda Argus*, 15 March 1969, page 3.
[2] Broome. *Library Work in Africa: Books for the People*. An experiment in library service in Tanganyika. Pages 69–70.

particular, when every claimant on the public purse knows that the grip and scrutiny of authority in all its forms is tightening, it is critical that a rationally presented case, soundly based in social terms, be made for libraries".[1] The Public Libraries Board cannot be an exception to this!

Uganda lacks the social, educational and philanthropic personalities which Ghana and Tanzania enjoyed. Ghana had a blessing in having Bishop Aglionby, who fought hard to convince the government of the importance of establishing public-library services in Ghana. In addition to making his personal stock available for the public's use, he also donated £1 000 for the development of libraries in Ghana. Mr. Karamjee, the Chairman of the Tanganyika Library Board, has proved a great source of help to the Tanganyika Library Service. Men like William Ewart in England, Von Rauner in Berlin, and Andrew Carnegie and J. Passmore in America did much to promote public-library services in their countries.

Uganda lacks such people at present, but its need is no less great for persons who are willing to preach the gospel of the library service as well as to give generously towards library development.

In addressing the Third East African Library Association Conference at Dar-es-Salaam in 1968, the Rev. T. T. T. Nabeta, the Vice-Chairman of the Public Libraries Board, who has devoted much energy to the development of public libraries in Uganda, showed that tremendous need and interest had been awakened in the people of Uganda but that there were still limited resources to fully satisfy the needs. He hoped that drastic measures would soon be taken to meet the situation and, indeed, such measures have been in evidence since then. For instance, a directive was given by the Ministry of Regional Administration to the effect that the local authorities at Mbale, Fort Portal, and Gulu should find the sum of 600 000 shillings each for the building of regional headquarters in those places. A one-man commission of inquiry was set up to investigate the present state of the library service and to recommend

---

[1] W. Caldwell. The library in the social structure, *The Assistant Librarian*, Vol. 61, No. 10, October, 1955, pages 249–253.

ways and means of improving it. The report has been handed to the Minister and a White Paper on it is expected, which, it is hoped, will set new guide-lines for the Public Libraries Board developments.

These are all steps taken in the proper direction and signs of good development in the future.

Bibliography

Wheeler, Joseph L. *Practical Administration of Public Libraries*, Joseph L. Wheeler and Herbert Ghodor. New York, Harper & Row, 1962. 517 pp.

Murison, W. J. *The Public Library: Its Origins, Purpose and Significance as a Social Institution*. London, George G. Harrap, 1955. 222 pp.

Evans, Evelyn J. A. *A Tropical Library Service; The Story of Ghana's Libraries*. London, Andre Deutsch, 1964. 172 pp.

UNESCO. *Development of Public Libraries in Africa; The Ibadan Seminar*. Paris, UNESCO, 1954. 153 pp.

Hockey, S. W. *Development of Library Services in East Africa*, A report submitted to the governments of East Africa, 1960.

McColvin, Lionel, R. *The Chance To Read; Public Libraries in the World Today*. London, Phoenix House, 1956. 284 pp.

Wallenius, Anna-Britta (ed.). *Library Work in Africa*. Upsala, Scandinavian Institute of African Studies, 1966. 75 pp.

Harrison, K. G. *Public Libraries Today*. London, Lockwood, 1963. 146 pp. (New Librarianship Series).

Annesley, G. *Survey of Library Provision for Africans in Kenya, Uganda, Tanganyika and Zanzibar, and Proposed Organisation for a Library Service for Africans*. Nairobi, E.A.L.B., 1948.

UNESCO. *The Public Library Manifesto:* The public library, a living force for popular education. Paris, 1948.

McColvin, Lionel, R. Public libraries. In the *Encyclopaedia of Librarianship* (1958). Pp. 249–253.

Uganda. *The Public Libraries Act (Rev. Ed.) 1964*. Entebbe, The Government Printer, 1964.

Serwadda, G. W. The development of public library service in Uganda. *East African Library Association Bulletin* (Nairobi), 7: 26–28. June, 1966.

Fiddes, P. Library go-ahead sought; 25 000 books and cash available. *Uganda Argus*, 19 June 1962, p. 4.

Uganda. Ministry of Culture and Community Development. Speech of the Minister of Culture and Community Development, read for him by the Commissioner of Community Development. *Uganda Argus,* 15 March 1969, p. 3.

Richards, G. The beginning of public library services in Uganda. *East African Library Association Bulletin* (Nairobi), 4: 3–5, June, 1963.

Uganda Library Service. *Annual Report for the Year 1964–65.* Kampala 1965.

Uganda Library Service. *Annual Report for the Year 1965–66.* Kampala 1966.

Uganda Library Service. *Annual Report for the Year Ending 30 June 1967.* Kampala 1967.

Uganda Library Service. Commission's Report on Library Services throughout Uganda. Kampala, 1968 (unpublished).

Tanganyika Library Service. *Annual Report 1965–66.* Dar-es-Salaam 1966.

Ghana Library Board. *Annual Report 1965.* Accra 1966.

East African Literature Bureau. *Annual Reports 1945–1956,* 6; 7–8; 13–16; 6–11; 2–6. Nairobi 1956.

East African Literature Bureau. *Annual Reports 1956–61,* 2–6; 2–6; 1–9; 1–9; 1–10; 2–10. Nairobi 1961.

East African Literature Bureau. *Annual Report 1961–62,* 3–10; 1–10; 4–8. Nairobi 1962.

Uganda Library Service. *Uganda Library Service Bulletin,* VI. Kampala, January, 1966.

Uganda Library Service. *Uganda Library Service Newsletter,* 1/68. Kampala, January/February 1968.

Nabeta, T. T. T. The Uganda Library Service; Paper presented at the Dar-es-Salaam East African Library Association Conference, 1968 (unpublished).

Serwadda, G. W. In my view. *East African Library Association Bulletin,* 5: 10–12. Nairobi, January, 1964.

S. W. Hockey

The Development of Library Services in East Africa

Most of the material in this symposium will consist of papers read at the Third Conference of the East African Library Association in September 1968, which should provide a fairly detailed picture of the present state of library development in East Africa. The purpose of this article, therefore, is to attempt a brief history of the evolution of these services and the principles upon which they are being established and to identify some of the problems facing them today, which, in many cases, have delayed the implementation of the plans adopted 10 years ago. Indeed, it may well be that the time has come when these plans should be re-examined in the light of the educational, social and economic changes which have taken place during the past 10 years.

The next conference in Uganda in 1970, which will possibly coincide with a projected UNESCO Conference on library planning and finance, should provide an opportunity for this exercise, and could prove to be another landmark in the history of library development in East Africa. We now have enough library services of all kinds in existence to provide a working background for a revised blue-print, if one is necessary, and, one would hope, a sufficient body of experience upon which to plan the next phase of development. We have certainly reached a stage when that well-worn and much-abused word "co-ordination" must be given another airing.

The first conference in Nairobi in 1957 was devoted mainly to the discussion of plans for the establishment of public-library services in Kenya, and the fact that the "East African"

Library Association consisted mainly of a small group of professional librarians in Kenya is indicative of the low status accorded to librarianship at that time. The only University Library in existence was that of Makerere College in Uganda and apart from a few good specialist and technical libraries (mainly in Kenya), East Africa could be described as a library wilderness, in which a few professional voices were crying for better things.

The public-library services consisted of a few subscription libraries, limited by the terms of reference under which they were established, and serving only selected sections of the community. The honourable exception to these were the libraries of the East African Literature Bureau, an organisation based in the East African High Commission (later the East African Common Services Organisation and now the East African Community), which were set up in the Bureau's headquarters in each territory, from which books were distributed throughout the area through postal and book-box services, and a few larger static collections. The Director of the Bureau had the foresight to secure the services of three qualified librarians to run these services (and by 1962 one of these was the first qualified African librarian) and the work of these people, with pitifully inadequate resources, can be said to have laid the foundations upon which the public-library services are now being built. It has not, I think, been fully recognised.

The 1961–2 Report of the Bureau showed an annual issue of about 150 000 books, a by no means insignificant figure in relation to the conditions prevailing at that time. During the course of an interview for a trainee post in the Kenya National Library Service, the applicant (a graduate) was asked why he was considering librarianship as a career. His reply was that he would not have achieved his present position without the help of the postal service, which kept him regularly supplied with books in the remote outpost in which he was serving, and that he felt that this was a worth-while job, in which he would like to participate. Book issues cannot always be assessed by quantity.

This may be an appropriate place to comment on the policy behind the establishment of the Bureau libraries, as it is one which needs constant reiteration in the development of library services in these countries. The Director already saw that, if the work of the Bureau, which was mainly concerned with basic literacy, was to have any lasting effect, it must be supported by library services, which would provide "follow-up" reading material for the people in the rural areas to whom the Bureau's publications were directed, thus conforming to the UNESCO dictum that library services must be firmly built into any campaign of mass education. One has to say, more in sorrow than in anger, that this farsightedness is all too rare. Over the years I have attended many conferences and read a great many reports dealing with programmes for adult education, community development and literacy campaigns. Seldom has the establishment of library services, which is surely the only way of ensuring the continuity of these programmes, received more than cursory attention. The programme of the Dar-es-Salaam Conference included a session on libraries and literacy and it is to be hoped that all those responsible for library development in East Africa will ensure that a close liaison is achieved between the library services and the work being done in the fields of literacy and adult education.

Many of the Literature Bureau book-boxes went to schools and the role of the national library services in the development of school libraries needs to be defined.

The long-awaited breakthrough in the establishment of public-library services in East Africa came in 1959, with a despatch from the Secretary of State for the Colonies to the East African Governments, offering capital aid to public-library services upon the acceptance by the Governments of viable plans for the initial establishment and development of such services. The area was surveyed, and plans of development were produced for each territory, which were accepted by the advisory committees set up for this purpose. The basic recommendations were that central or national services should be set up, which, from a headquarters in the capital city, should be responsible for the establishment, maintenance and development of library services on a territorial basis. They were to be under the control of statutory Library Boards which were to be given wide powers. The libraries of the East African Literature Bureau were to be absorbed into the new national libraries.

What progress has been made during the past 10 years? Those who have studied the history of library development in any part of the world or who have been involved in the struggle to secure recognition of library services as an essential component of cultural and educational advancement will not need to be told of the obstacles which have been encountered in launching these services in East Africa. One only has to look back on the early history of British county libraries, many of which, after the initial injection of Carnegie aid, stagnated for years due to the lack of interest on the part of the education authorities, who are not always by any means our most enlightened supporters.

During the early years of this decade the East African Governments were pre-occupied with rapid and drastic political changes, and with all the legislation that these involved, it was surprising that the acts establishing the Library Boards got into the Statute Book during the first five years; one might say, cynically, more perhaps by default than by any great show of enthusiasm for these projects. Owing to the many changes in the ministry responsible for the service, the Kenya Library Board was not effectively established until 1967, and it is only this year that the national library service has secured reasonable provision in the territorial estimates, together with the acceptance of a five-year development plan. The Uganda Library Board has been equally unsuccessful in securing adequate recurrent expenditure, and for the last two years has been without a book fund. Nevertheless the services are in existence, and even the limited work which is being done is creating public support and demands for services which will, inevitably, force the governments to recognise them.

The one exception to this gloomy picture is to be found in Tanzania, where, the other territorial services must reluctantly agree, the development of the national services has forged ahead with remarkable speed and efficiency. East Africa is fortunate in possessing, in the form of the Tanganyika Library Service, a model of library development, and a working base for the purposes of experimentation and evaluation.

In an article in the *Scandinavian Public Library Quarterly* (Vol. 1: 3, 1968) Sigvard Möhlenbrock admirably defined the criteria for successful library planning, and as these criteria are very relevant to the needs of East Africa, it is worth repeating them here:

1. Foreseeing and preparing for new situations likely to arise and seeing that the right things and not the wrong things happen.
2. Seeing that the library, the trustees, the librarian and the staff do not get pushed around, but that the library has a programme worked out, and that it prevails, despite external and internal delays and pressures.
3. Identifying a problem and defining and limiting its coverage, while discovering more and more of its component elements and its consequences.
4. Calling on the help of one or a few colleagues best qualified in the matter at hand for frequent conferences to analyse the problem or proposal and its parts and to outline a detailed course of action.
5. Seeing to it that planning is not so weak and long-drawn-out or aims at such perfection that nothing gets done.

The second requirement will raise a wry smile in some parts of East Africa.

The Tanganyika Library Service was fortunate in securing, from its inception, brilliant direction, supported by a qualified and experienced staff, an active Board and, as a consequence, the support of the government and the donors of capital aid. It has matched speed of development with careful planning at each stage and from its headquarters, group and branch libraries (many of them delightful new buildings), it is now ready to extend its services to the rural areas. Particular attention is being paid to these areas by the government, and in some interesting articles in the Library Service's house journal some of the staff criticised the provision of "western-style" buildings and book stock as being expensive luxuries unrelated to the essential work of the services. This is a fallacy. The organisation of an adequate service to scattered communities is a relatively expensive and complicated job, and it can only be done effectively by first establishing well-organised and properly equipped bases, from which the tenuous network of mobile stops and village centres can be supplied and supervised. This will become apparent as the work progresses.

The plans for the national library services envisaged that, apart from the organisation of public library services, they would eventually assume the following additional responsibilities:

(1) The acquisition and exploitation of a national collection, including the material acquired by legal deposit.

(2) The organisation of government departmental libraries and any other specialist libraries requiring such assistance.

(3) The organisation of school library services in co-operation with the Ministries of Education.

The Tanganyika Library Service has already begun to plan the extension of its services along these lines, and has called for expert surveys on departmental and schools library services.

This all conforms to the basic administrative principle that only a large and well-organised central organisation can provide the facilities to ensure an overall standard of efficiency, thus avoiding the proliferation of small and ill-equipped services and the consequent dissipation of limited resources which have hindered progress in many of the advanced countries. This golden opportunity will, however, be lost if the national library services cannot rapidly build up the resources, particularly of trained staff, which will enable them to meet the many demands being made upon them. If these requests for help cannot be met, many of the authorities concerned will "go it alone". This is particularly true in the most important field of schools library services, and with the tremendous increase in the numbers of pupils in secondary and primary schools, this is becoming an urgent problem.

The other most important development during the period under review has, of course, been the founding of the two University Libraries in Dar-es-Salaam and Nairobi. The University Libraries, with their splendid buildings and equipment, are often the envy of their professional brethren, in that their place in the University is recognised from the beginning (the library is usually the first building to be erected) and although, like librarians the world over, they complain of lack of funds, they do not have to suffer many of the vicissitudes of those trying to squeeze money out of reluctant Treasuries in the early stages of the development of public-library services. Moreover, although they would stoutly deny it, they receive more generous overseas aid through the endowments to the University, which is naturally in a stronger position to attract support of this kind.

The University Libraries, which are geared to the requirements of academic institutions, obviously have a distinct and limited function to perform. Nevertheless they are making their impact upon the professional scene outside of the campus, and in each territory the University Librarian is a member of the National Library Board; at this stage of development in East Africa librarians cannot afford to isolate themselves in specialist groups. It is to be hoped that the co-operation between the University Libraries and the national services will continue to expand, particularly in the development of bibliographical services, which are sadly lacking in East Africa at the moment.

All the reports on the East African Library Services will indubitably mention the one factor which, more than any other, is hampering library development in East Africa, and that is the lack of qualified and experienced staff. Again, if one considers the long struggle to secure the recognition of librarianship as a profession in Europe and America, this must be accepted as inevitable. It is, however, unfortunate that this problem has not been tackled by those responsible for the provision of capital aid to library services (although it has often been aired at conferences) and that it has not been possible to match capital aid with the provision of trained staff to launch the projects set up in this way.

The need to initiate a rapid and intensive programme of training for Africans was clearly foreseen in the 1960 Report, and the establishment of an East African School of Librarianship was recommended. A conference sponsored by the Rockefeller Foundation in 1968 endorsed this recommendation and it was decided that a School of Librarianship should be set up at Makerere College which would run a Certificate Course for new entrants to the profession and a two-year Diploma Course which would qualify candidates for serious professional posts. Unfortunately, the hopes that the Rockefeller Foundation would set up the School as a complete entity, including the provision of staff, did not materialise, but with the appointment of a Director by the UNESCO in 1963 and with assistance from various sources, the School has struggled along and at last appears to be firmly established. During the period 1964–8 the School awarded 79 Certificates in Librarianship and 17 Diplomas.

The subject of training for librarianship in East Africa has been fully dealt with in a paper submitted at the conference by the Director and no elaboration of the problems facing those engaged in this work is needed here. Suffice it to say that a strong indigenous training school, which can orientate its training programme to the particular needs of East Africans and which, apart from formal training, can contribute a great deal in research and related fields, must be regarded as an essential institution.

This paper is written by a Libraries Organiser who is just completing nine years of deep involvement in the battle to establish library services in East Africa—a battle which is being fought in fierce competition for the limited funds available to the governments for the rapid expansion of educational and social services at all levels to which they are committed. It is to be expected that it will conclude, therefore, with a plea for the continuation of the generous assistance which has been provided by the overseas governments, who fully recognise the value of this work. In particular, we would like to see more librarians coming out to help us. Not the experts who come for a few weeks to sketch the grand designs, but the journeymen who are prepared to help to dig the foundations and lay some bricks.

S. S. Saith

The East African School of Librarianship: Past, Present and Future

Now seems to be an appropriate time to present a paper on the East African School of Librarianship, because the School has passed the stage of mere existence and has arrived at a point where it is beginning to fulfil its proper role in the development of the three East African countries. I have attempted to sketch the motives behind the creation of this regional institution, the chequered history, and the recent developments, and to estimate the success of the School up to date. I have also indicated the present and future requirements of the School.

The realization that local training for African librarians was an integral part of any plan for the development of the library services in East Africa came in 1960. At this time, a report on the development of library services on a national basis was submitted to the three Governments of East Africa.[1] This initiative was taken by the British Council and is one of their many pioneering steps in bringing the significant aspects of modern civilization to developing areas. Like the UNESCO, the British Council has shown its abiding faith in the role which books and libraries have to play in the educational, social, and economic development of all the people of the earth. The Report included a strong recommendation for the establishment of an East African School of Librarianship.

An advisory committee was then appointed by the three East

[1] *Development of Library Services in East Africa:* A Report Submitted to the Governments of East Africa by S. W. Hockey, British Council Libraries Organiser in East Africa. Nairobi, December 1960. 42 pp.

African governments to consider the report. It was decided that funds could be found only for the recurring expenditure needed to set up the new national library services. The establishment of a school of librarianship was thought to be beyond the financial means of the three Governments, particularly as the British Council was also unable to help by providing a Director for the proposed School.

The next tangible moves were in 1963, when the report attracted the attention of the UNESCO, the world body concerned with the development of education at all levels. The UNESCO gave fresh impetus to the establishment of the School by agreeing to provide a Director. The Rockefeller Foundation also showed its interest by offering to assist the School as part of its aid to the University of East Africa. As a first step, the Rockefeller Foundation financed a library training conference in Nairobi in April 1963. The conference was attended by representatives of the East African Governments, prominent librarians from East Africa and representatives from overseas library organizations, including the UNESCO. The conference set up a working party, which, *inter alia,* again recommended to the East African Governments that an East African School of Librarianship should be established. It was suggested that it should be under the auspices of the University of East Africa at a college designated by the University. The conference further recommended that the proposed School should conduct two courses: firstly, a Certificate Course in library methods for library assistants, and secondly a two-year Diploma Course, which would qualify candidates for professional posts in libraries.

The oldest of the three constituent colleges of the University of East Africa, namely, Makerere University College, Kampala, indicated its interest in the project, and offered the School its hospitality. Responding to this initiative, the Senate of the University of East Africa delegated the responsibility for the School to Makerere University College and recommended the creation of a body to be known as the Council for Library Training in East Africa (CLTEA) to supervise the School and the adoption of regulations for the School, subject to the agreements of the East African Governments and the East African

Community. As a result of these developments, the UNESCO formally appointed Professor Knud Larsen, who had been a participant in the Nairobi Conference as the Director of the School in 1963. This appointment of a Director was the first practical step towards the founding of the East African School of Librarianship.

The College has been established as a separate university and known as Makerere University since 1 July 1970. It is composed of eight major faculties and four institutes and schools. The two main features of the present structure which are worth noting are that the School of Librarianship is independent of the faculties, and that the supervision of the School is entrusted to the CLTEA, which has representatives from all the three countries. This composition of the CLTEA safeguards the status of the School as a regional institution. The CLTEA is an independent body responsible to the Makerere University Senate. Its functions are identical with those of a faculty board, and the School has a certain degree of autonomy, which simplifies the administrative procedures and which is necessary to accelerate the pace of the School's development on a regional basis.

In September 1968, the East African Community set up a Working Party on Higher Education to consider the likelihood that, at some time after the triennial planning period ending on 30 June 1970, the three constituent colleges of the University of East Africa at Kampala, Nairobi, and Dar-es-Salaam would be replaced by three or more separate universities. A memorandum was submitted to the Working Party by the present Director of the School in September 1968, urging it to allow the School to continue as a regional institution.[2] The Working Party recommended that the three universities should co-operate in providing and maintaining certain duplicated facilities, such as the East African School of Librarianship. The report proposed that a new body, to be known as the Inter-

---

[2] Makerere University College. East African School of Librarianship. Memorandum submitted to the East African Community Working Party on Higher Education by the Director of the School. Kampala: September 1968. 8 pp.

University Committee for East Africa, should be created for this purpose, and the School of Librarianship was mentioned as one of the non-duplicated facilities.[3]

After stating that "We do not wish to set down guidelines for specialisation, preferring to leave it for discussion among the Universities and Governments", the Working Party made a specific recommendation with regard to the School of Librarianship in the following words, a recommendation which has since been accepted by the East African Authority:

> We recommend in the case of the professional training of librarians that the East African School of Librarianship at Makerere University College should continue to serve all three states on a regional basis after the dissolution of the University of East Africa, until circumstances warrant a review.[4]

This decision of the East African Committee was further endorsed by the Visitation Committee to the Makerere University College before the College assumed full university status as a national university on 1 July 1970.[5]

My only concern regarding the School as a regional institution is whether the other two governments will accept financial responsibility for the capital development and maintenance of *any* non-duplicated facility. If they do not, and no suggestion appears to have been made in the Working Party report that they should, then this will be a great personal disappointment, because the terms of reference of the Working Party had raised a hope that the financial arrangements would also be recommended.

It has been mentioned earlier that it was Makerere University College which offered hospitality to the School. Anyone who is familiar with the rapid development which has occurred at the College since Uganda gained its independence in Octo-

---

[3] East African Community Report of the Working Party on Higher Education in East Africa submitted to the East African Authority at Arusha. Nairobi: 31 January 1969, p. 68.

[4] Ibid., p. 39.

[5] Uganda. Report of the Visitation Committee to Makerere University College, submitted to His Excellency Dr. A. Milton Obote, M.P., President of the Republic of Uganda, Visitor to Makerere University College. Entebbe: Government Printer, June 1970, p. 47.

ber 1962 will realise the keen competition which has existed between all departments, both old and new, for the allocation of funds. As the School was being set up at the request of the three East African governments, the College felt that proportionate funds should be made available by the three countries. It was also hopeful that a particular external agency would provide funds to help the establishment of the School. It would appear that the School failed to press its claim for allocation of the necessary funds for the School from the three governments, and it may well be that the initial interest expressed by the external agency flagged because of the slow rate of the School's progress. In short, the arrangements envisaged for financing the School did not materialise.

Nor could the School be inducted into the financial structure of the College, partly for administrative reasons, and partly, I suspect, because the College clung to the hope that the School would be able to attract funds from external agencies. Nevertheless the College provided it with an office, teaching accommodation, and housing for the Director and the students; furthermore it paid certain administrative expenses. But the School languished for lack of funds in the same way that many a Carnegie library has done in the United Kingdom. It maintained a semblance of existence on sporadic gifts of money from external agencies and with the meagre support of the College.

In spite of considerable teething troubles, however, it is significant that the School has survived. This was due to the fact that, when the infant institution was uncertain of its future, it received valuable and timely contributions from different external agencies which staked their faith in the future of the School.

The British Council has aided the School in many ways from its inception in 1963. This aid has taken the form of cash donations to meet office expenses, books, recurring funds for the award of bursaries to the students, and the expenses of their attendance at library conferences. Also Sidney Hockey, the British Council Libraries Organizer in East Africa, having fathered the idea of establishing the School of Librarianship, made persistent efforts during the period between 1960 and

1969 to ensure its success. The School owes a great debt to him for his dedication, and his highly efficient assistance through a very difficult period. In July 1969, the British Council, as a result of energetic efforts made by Sidney Hockey and Roy Flood, yet another friend of the School at the British Council headquarters in London, provided a Visiting Lecturer to the School for one year. This provision was later extended for a further year.

The Rockefeller Foundation financed the Nairobi Conference on Library Training in April 1963, and thus helped in establishing the School. Subsequently, it provided a Lecturer and secretarial assistance for a year.

The Danish Government has aided the School consistently and generously since 1965, when Professor Knud Larsen, the first Director provided by the UNESCO, brought the School to the attention of his Government. In 1965 it provided the School with a Danish Lecturer, and this aid continues to this day. In 1967, when the School was beset with serious staffing situation, it was the Danish Government again which increased its technical assistance by providing another Lecturer for a period of two years.

Although Professor Larsen could not continue to give the benefit of his talent and experience to the East African School of Librarianship beyond 1965 for personal reasons, he has continued to project the needs of the School whenever there has been a suitable opportunity. In 1965 he tried to arouse and stimulate the interest of Swedish librarians in the School in the following words when he addressed the Conference on "Library Work in Africa" held in Norrköping on 30–31 August 1965:

But I take this conference as evidence of Sweden's intention to extend its assistance to African libraries. Therefore I suggest a quick rescue operation to bring the School out of this deadlock.

The reason why we are here is that we are deeply interested in the future of Africa, and hope you all agree with me that this scheme (i.e. the School of Librarianship at Makerere) has a higher priority in the help we are to offer to Africa.[6]

[6] Knud Larsen, Librarians and library training in East Africa, in *Library Work in Africa*. Uppsala 1966, p. 38.

In 1967, the Swedish librarians and library readers raised £1 212 sterling by voluntary contributions for the award of three bursaries to the students of the Certificate Course in Library Studies as a gesture of their interest in the School of Librarianship. Two years later the School received a further gift from Sweden of U.S. $6 575 for the award of scholarships in librarianship "as a proof of the importance which the Swedish public librarians put on the training offered by the School of Librarianship". These donations, collected from librarians and library readers during fund-raising campaigns organised by the Swedish Public Libraries Association, demonstrate the very practical assistance being given to the School by Sweden. Even more important, they show the interest and concern which Sweden has for the success of the library profession in East Africa.

I have not been able to research adequately to set out the precise nature and extent of all the contributions provided by external agencies. This inventory of aid is, therefore, by no means complete. However, judging from the nature and diversity of this aid, every single contribution has been useful, and has helped the School to survive. Without these continuous and timely rescue operations, the School could not have continued to function.

The UNESCO has aided the School since its inception in March 1963. The aid to the School has been mainly limited to providing the services of a Director, and funds for the purchase of books and equipment. During the period 1965–1967, the School was aided by the UNESCO under the UNDP Country Programme of Technical Assistance. This Programme required the host country to determine the priorities of the projects which it wished to finance from UNDP funds, each country receiving a certain allocation for its development. Under the Country Programme, the host country also determines the extent of the assistance with regard to the number of the UNESCO experts required to man the project and its duration.

In 1967, realizing the slow rate of progress made by the School, the UNESCO got the project transferred from the UNDP Country Programme to the Regional Programme from the biennium 1967–1968. This was done with the object of planning assistance to the School on a long-term basis, and on a larger scale, according to the UNDP's own assessment of the needs. From the biennium 1969–1970, the UNESCO has increased the allocation of funds for the purchase of equipment and continued to provide a Director but raised his status to make it compatible with the increasing responsibilities developed by the project. It has also provided funds for a fellowship, so that an East African citizen can be trained as a counterpart Director or as a Lecturer, if no suitable candidate for the Director's post is available. Now that the East African School of Librarianship has been placed under the UNDP Regional Programme, it merely requires the expression of support from the three countries of the region for the UNDP to continue its aid. It does not affect the allocation of funds given to the three countries of the region under Country Programmes.

It is certain that the UNESCO assistance to the School will be continued during the next biennium 1971–1972. But I believe that this is an excellent time for the UNESCO to increase its assistance to the School by providing another expert to support the Director in the tasks that lie ahead. In view of the importance which the UNESCO attaches to the project, this course of action would set the seal on the future of the School. Moreover this also accords with two of the recommendations contained in the UNESCO Committee's report on the evaluation of its aided projects in Africa, which read as follows:

This School has a regional role to play in East Africa in the training of fully qualified librarians. The Committee recommends that UNESCO should continue to assist it to play this role ... UNESCO should increase its assistance to the School by providing one lecturer as well as a director, and the equipment ...[7]

---

[7] The UNESCO Regional Centre for the Training of Librarians from East African Countries, Makerere College, Uganda, in *UNESCO's Inter-African Programme*. Report of the Committee on the Evaluation of UNESCO-operated or -aided Regional Offices, Centres and Institutes in Africa. Paris: UNESCO, May 1968, p. 87.

In view of the UNESCO's considerable contribution towards developing the School of Librarianship to date, coupled with the fact that the College has more than met its own obligations, as will be seen presently, it is hoped that the UNESCO will be able to implement the recommendations of its Committee.

I now turn to the School's academic courses. From the end of 1963 to July 1965 the School conducted only Certificate Courses in Library Studies. It would appear that the teaching was done by the founder Director of the School and one tutor provided by the Rockefeller Foundation. In July 1965, however, the School decided to start a two-year Diploma Course in Librarianship, which had to be lengthened by one year, as the students did not meet the University's entrance qualifications and were therefore required to do a year of general studies. The students who joined the second Diploma Course in 1966 did not fare any better.

The year 1967 marks the beginning of the second phase of library education at Makerere for two reasons. In 1967 Makerere decided that the students who passed the Certificate in Library Studies with Honours but who, nevertheless, lacked university entrance qualifications would be admitted to the Diploma in Librarianship course on obtaining the Certificate of Adult Studies awarded by the Centre of Continuing Education at Makerere or an equivalent qualification from the University Colleges in Nairobi or Dar-es-Salaam. This therefore dispensed with the need to have general studies incorporated into the Diploma, which then became a two-year course of professional studies.

The third phase of the School can be said to have started with the academic year 1968–69. When the present Director joined Makerere in July 1968, the staff of the School consisted of two Danish Lecturers fully funded by the Danish Government and a British Lecturer occupying the only Lecturer post provided by the College. This staff was insufficient to implement the School's full training programmes. The CLTEA had made a specific recommendation to the College, based on the report of the External Examiner, that, for the Diploma course alone, the School should have a staff of six members.

But despite persistent efforts by the CLTEA, the College did not establish the requisite number of posts on the ground that the development of library training at the School had proceeded at a slow pace, though this was inevitable because of the various factors.

It was obvious that, in order to press the School's claim in the university community for any increase in funds or staff, and to impress the College with the future possibilities of the School, it would have to win recognition for its work and demonstrate the School as a flourishing institution. There was therefore no escape from planning to implement the School's full programmes with the existing staff of three members. A description of the three programmes, which the School began fully to undertake from the academic session 1968–69, is given below:

(*a*) *Certificate Course in Library Studies.* This is an intensive six-month course in library techniques and methods for library assistants holding a School Certificate. Although the Course is chiefly concerned with the practical aspects of librarianship, a good deal of attention is given to teaching the basic principles underlying library techniques and skills. The selection of candidates takes into account the value of their library experience. Gradually the entry qualifications of this Course have been raised to the point at which only those candidates who have passed the School Certificate with five credits are now admitted to the Course.

(*b*) *Diploma Course in Librarianship.* A two-year course of professional studies for undergraduates, leading to the award of a Diploma in Librarianship, which is a basic qualification for professional librarians. The candidates seeking admission must meet the general entrance requirements of the University to study for any degree or must have passed a Mature Age Entry Examination of the University, the standard of which is rigorously high.

(*c*) *Introductory Library Studies Course.* This course is given to all the students already admitted in the Faculty of Education for the degree of Bachelor of Education as a part of their education syllabus within the present structure of the B.Ed.

programme. The students receive three hours' instruction a week for one term.

The overall objective is to demonstrate the place of the library in the school and to outline some of the elementary techniques and skills used for inculcating the reading habit and the use of library materials by the pupils at different levels.

(*d*) In addition to the regular programmes described above, the School was able to make a very significant contribution to a three-month UNESCO/Friedrich Naumann Foundation Regional Training Course in Documentation, conducted under the auspices of the School in 1969. Fourteen students from Kenya, Malawi, Tanzania, Uganda, and Zambia, including three ex-Diploma students from our own School, with experience in documentation work or librarianship, participated in the course. The course was financed by the Friedrich Naumann Foundation (West Germany), which provided Visiting Lecturers for a period of one or two weeks, while one Lecturer provided by the School of Librarianship acted as a part-time instructor as well as co-ordinator for the duration of the course.

When the School undertook to launch all of its three programmes in 1968–69, as envisaged in its founding objectives, it was hoped that the teaching strength of four members, which included the Director, would be augmented by a Visiting Lecturer from the British Council. While the British Council Lecturer materialised, the staffing situation did not improve, for one of the two Lecturers provided by the Danish Government left on the expiry of his contract, and the earnest efforts made by the Danish Government to send his replacement did not bear fruit.

Similarly, efforts made by the School to ask the College for an increase in the figures budgeted for the triennium 1968–70 on the grounds that the implementation of the full programme of the School from the academic year 1968–69 had considerably altered the School's anticipated budgetary expenditure for the remaining two years of the triennial period 1968–70 did not succeed, due to procedural difficulties. Inevitably we had to resign ourselves to wait for the next triennial budget 1970–73. The School's work, however, helped to focus the attention of the Makerere authorities on the need to assume responsibility for establishing all the academic posts and an adequate budget, which would allow the School to function properly and plan its future with certainty.

On the basis of the actual and projected training programmes and in accordance with the principles of planning, the Makerere authorities have accepted the main arguments of the School's development for the triennium 1970–73.[8] The University has established five permanent academic posts, including that of the Director, funds for which have been provided from the end of December 1972, when the UNESCO aid to the School is likely to cease. It has also made a generous provision in the budget for part-time teachers (if available), permanent secretarial staff, office expenses, stores and equipment, as requested in the Development Plan beginning with the academic year 1970–71.

Thus, after an arduous struggle the School of Librarianship has finally been integrated into the structure of Makerere University, in spite of the many pressures on its resources. The final result achieved is gratifying and we should not concern ourselves too much with the time taken to achieve it.

The UNESCO Committee on the evaluation of its aided projects in Africa had visited the School in November 1967 and had observed in its report that "the administration of the School is housed in very inadequate premises, which give the Director an office which is little larger than a cupboard". Strenuous efforts were made to improve the situation, and in October 1968 the College's concern for the proper functioning of the School was reflected in its decision to house the School in the new mathematics/science building. The temporary accommodation consists of three offices, two lecture rooms which are shared with the Mathematics Department, and a Seminar Room in the College Library for the exclusive use of our students. This is, of course, a vast improvement on the previous accommodation.

For the proper functioning of the School it was essential to

---

[8] Makerere University College, East African School of Librarianship, Development Plan for 1970–73. Kampala: August 1963. 10 pp.

have a permanent building, but funds for the building could not be expected from the College's resources. The choice was either to continue to cope with a recurring accommodation problem or to strive for a permanent solution by securing funds from an external agency. Informal negotiations with a certain donor country which had shown interest in the School were set in motion in 1969. Since then all possible efforts have been expended to secure the capital funds. An evaluative paper on the various aspects of the School was prepared, followed by a submission of a formal application at the request of the country.

The application gave estimates of the accommodation needed for the School's administration, the members of the School's faculty, teaching space, and a library. The library has been provided for the twofold purpose of giving supervised library practice to future direct entrants to the Diploma Course, who will not have previous library experience, and for two of the other programmes, which place special emphasis on the practical aspects of librarianship.

Negotiations have been conducted on both sides in the spirit of the motto of Makerere University, "We build for the future", and I am confident that the country will be able to put this into concrete action, and provide the necessary funds.

Meanwhile, following the visit of the country's library adviser to Kampala, a fine site has been allocated for the School's building, adjacent to the University Library. What is still more significant, the Uganda Government has agreed to advance a loan to Makerere University for the construction of the long-awaited building, in the hope that the donor country will be able to provide the funds. This favourable development, however, is yet another proof of the concern of the Makerere University and the Uganda Government to meet the School's pressing needs and to secure its future. Thus, in spite of many difficulties, the building is now in prospect.

The fact that the School of Librarianship has not yet been able to appoint a single African Lecturer to its staff has been a matter of grave concern to me. I have raised this subject with the Makerere authorities and the CLTEA at every possible opportunity since joining the School. Although it is recognised on all hands that no satisfactory solution to the School's future can be foreseen unless it can recruit African staff, no imminent solution is foreseeable. Consequently the School has continued to rely entirely on overseas countries to provide the staff. Librarianship is a new discipline in East Africa and it has not yet reached such a stage of recognition as to attract persons of suitable calibre, interested in obtaining good academic qualifications and an advanced degree in librarianship for the purpose of taking up teaching as a career.

For the same reason the School was not able to avail itself of the offer made by the former University of East Africa early in 1969 to appoint an African Lecturer for a period of two years from Special Lecturership Programme funds created by the University, regardless of whether or not the School had an established post in its budget.

The UNESCO attaches great importance to training local staff, who will be able to carry on the work of managing the project when the UNESCO aid to it ceases. Consequently, the UNESCO provided a fellowship for a period of one year for training a counterpart Director or a Lecturer, if a suitable candidate for the Director's post could not be found. This UNESCO fellowship is tenable for one year, and is meant to enable a person who already possesses basic professional qualifications to pursue a formal course of higher studies and to broaden his experience through a programme of professional observation and study. It is regrettable that, despite all the earnest and energetic efforts in this direction, the School has not been able to find a suitable candidate so far.

In the absence of established posts, the School has had to depend upon the donor countries to provide the staff. Makerere University has now established its own academic posts. However, the School will still continue to look to overseas countries for staff, for the reasons explained above, but with this vital difference, that the lecturers will work in the established posts financed by the University.

Recently Makerere University has diversified its recruitment policies, and I am confident that we will be able to attract staff who wish to accept the challenge of making a contribution to the development of the librarian's profession in this part of the world, which offers at the same time all the modern amenities, a superb climate, and a magnificent scenery.

The basic conditions for the development of an educational institution such as ours are the right staff, the right type of entrants for its programmes, funds and proper facilities. These are accordingly the factors on which not only the growth of the institution but also the rate of its progress depend.

One of our immediate needs is to seek bursaries for our students. Until now admission to our professional programme was required to be sponsored by the libraries which gave the candidates practical experience and sent them to our School on bursaries. Our experience for the past two years has shown that either the libraries are unable to attract apprentices with the required educational qualifications or they are unable to secure funds from their respective governments for bursaries. To give the fresh school-leavers the opportunity to take up the library profession, and thereby to provide the trained manpower needed for the development of libraries, the School is also now admitting fresh entrants, for whom it will arrange a specially devised and supervised library practice as a part of their training programme.

The governments of the three countries have a system of allocating bursaries for students who wish to pursue various professional courses. The national governments of the region also provide bursaries for training librarians, but it is being done on an *ad hoc* basis. I have no doubt that the governments will recognise the need for the fair allocation of funds and work out a system for this purpose in the long run, but this is not the fact at present.

I should like to express the opinion that it is necessary for the librarian's profession to support the School's efforts to persuade the governments to recognise the facts that (*a*) the need for trained staff is inherent in the very functions of a library, (*b*) only those libraries which have trained library personnel at different levels under the charge of a professional librarian can play an essential role in the social and economic development programmes of the region, and (*c*) among the many tasks devolving upon them by reason of their very broad responsibilities for the development of education, the allocation of funds for the training of librarians must be taken into account in planning priorities.

Now that the School of Librarianship has fulfilled many of its dreams, and has come to stay as a permanent landmark in the history of librarianship in East Africa, it can now enter a new phase of its development.

During this new phase, the School should redefine the objectives of its existing training programmes, recast and modernise the syllabi in the light of the latest developments in librarianship, and expand the School's functions to introduce courses with the object of training manpower for all categories of library personnel in East Africa, and not only for personnel at junior and intermediate levels.

Since joining the School, I have canvassed support for training graduate librarians, first on the occasion of my address to the East African Library Association Conference at Dar-es-Salaam held in September 1968, and more recently in my memorandum submitted to the Visitation Committee to Makerere University College before the College assumed the status of a University in July 1970. The Visitation Committee has also lent the weight of its authority by commending the proposal to Makerere University.

An even more compelling reason for the introduction of this programme is that the preference for graduate librarians is now being reflected increasingly in the recruitment policies of the University and national library services in East Africa, for which the candidates from all the three countries are being sent abroad for the necessary professional training.

Secondly, I believe it is generally agreed that one of the ways of raising the standard of secondary education and teacher training is to improve and develop the library services. The most effective method of accomplishing this is to employ teacher librarians. There is a great need to improve the competence of teacher librarians.

Our present course in Introductory Library Studies for all the students at the Faculty of Education preparing for the Bachelor of Education degree is given as a part of their education syllabus. It cannot aim at producing teacher librarians, because the students' heavy curriculum will not permit it. There is therefore an urgent need for the School to institute a full-time course in school librarianship of a standard comparable to similar courses leading to the Teacher Librarians Certificate awarded in developed countries for qualified teachers who wish to be placed in charge of secondary-school libraries.

Finally the School should institute special courses of short duration in public, university and special librarianship for those who have received basic professional education, to equip them for professional duties at a senior level in public, university and special libraries.

No educational institution can flourish without the co-operation of the profession it serves. These are times when librarianship is expanding everywhere. This is particularly true in Africa, where the profession is at a stage in which it is full of promise. This is therefore a time of great opportunity for the leaders of the profession in East Africa. I ask them to give all support to their School of Librarianship, now firmly established, so that, working together, we may serve the cause of education by building a strong body of professional librarians.

J. D. Pearson

African Bibliography since the Nairobi Conference

The International Conference on African Bibliography, held at University College, Nairobi, on 4–8 December 1967, was organized by the International African Institute and paid for with a grant generously supplied by the Ford Foundation. A report by the Chairman and Secretary of the Conference, J. D. Pearson and Ruth Jones, which was published in the Institute's journal *Africa* (vol. XXXVIII, no. 3, July 1968, pp. 293–331) and in a French summarized version in *Cahiers d'études africaines* (34, vol. IX, 1969, 2e cahier, pp. 318–336),[1] attempts to bring out the main points in the papers contributed by delegates and others and those made in discussion during the conference. The English version gives the names of participants and the titles of papers contributed by participants and others, as well as the English text of the recommendations.

Short reports on the Conference were published by Valerie Bloomfield (*Library materials on Africa*, V, 3, March 1968) and H. J. Scholz (*Afrika-Archiv*, Munich, 15 February 1968): Angela Molnos gave utterance to some "afterthoughts" in *East Africa journal*, February 1968. A few comments on the report, from Rhodesia, were made by E. E. B[urke] in *Rhodesian librarian* (I, 3, pp. 78–79): these were to some extent refuted by me in a talk given to the Mashonaland Branch of the

---

[1] The French translation of the recommendations passed by the Conference appeared in the same journal (32, vol. VIII, 1968, 4e cahier, pp. 642–645).

Rhodesia Library Association and reported in the same journal (I, 4, pp. 111–112).

At the Commonwealth Foundation Conference of Commonwealth Africa University Librarians, held at Lusaka in August 1969, a resolution was passed to the effect that African university libraries and other interested parties should report all developments in African bibliography, archival work, librarianship, and similar topics which emanate from, or are in the spirit of, the Nairobi resolutions, to the Secretariat of the International Conference on African Bibliography. The Secretariat is requested to issue information on these developments from time to time.

The Survey of Current Bibliographical Services

The full text of the papers submitted will be published by Frank Cass, of London, in the spring of 1970: the volume, to be issued under the obvious title of *The Bibliography of Africa,* will also contain the *Survey of current bibliographical services on Africa,* prepared for the Conference by its Secretary, Ruth Jones, and incorporating the gist of some 100 replies from 14 African and 17 other countries to a questionnaire sent to compilers of bibliographies and directors of bibliographical services in 1967 with some later additions.

The *Survey* owed its genesis to the reasons originally advanced for recommending the holding of the conference by its predecessor, the Tropical African Studies Conference at Ibadan, 1964, which felt that, in the words of Dr. Porter, President of the Nairobi Conference, "one of the problems to be considered was the duplication of effort, and the ways and means of avoiding this and achieving greater coordination and standardization". Though this feature was largely lost sight of and the results achieved under this head were minimal, it did in fact bring about a confrontation and agreement to co-operate between the two large-scale purveyors of card services, CIDESA and CARDAN, and other smaller agreements.

A study[2] made of the *Survey* (probably one of the first of many such destined to be made by students at library schools and others), entirely unaided by computer "hardware" or "software", but nevertheless carried out in the course of an hour or two, reveals the following interesting facts in respect of types of bibliography recorded.

The services fall fairly neatly into the following nine types:

1. *National Bibliographies*

I use the term "national" to mean bibliographies which list the books and other publications of a given country. These may be for African countries, in which case they list everything published in the country, irrespective of whether it is concerned with that country or the rest of Africa or not, and they exist for Ethiopia (Eth 1–1), Madagascar (Mad 1), Malawi (Mal 1), Nigeria (Nig Ib–1, Nig 2–1), Rhodesia, Senegal (Sen 1), South Africa (SA 1–1, 2 and SA CT 1–1), and Sierra Leone (S. L. 1). (Lists of the publications of Kenya, Tanzania, Uganda and Zambia are included in accessions lists issued by university libraries in each of the countries.) They may enumerate publications relating to Africa in countries outside that continent, as do Ger 1, UK 2 and US (St) 1. The first of these includes all publications in the German language issued in the two parts of Germany, Austria, Switzerland and South Africa; the second, in addition to books and articles, theses submitted to universities for higher degrees and indexes to references to Africa made during debates and other business in both Houses of Parliament and reported in Hansard, the official record of parliamentary proceedings. US (St) 1 covers also the publications of Canada. Not included in Miss Jones's survey is *Literatura o stranakh Azii i Afriki,* a Russian annual publication listing work on Asia and Africa.

---

[2] The study was based on the original sheets distributed to those attending the Conference and to some other persons: this original version differs somewhat from that published in the printed volume of proceedings and papers, some few entries being re-numbered and the following omitted entirely: Ang 1–2, 1–3, Fr 9, 12–2, Ger 2, 3, Nig (1b)2, SA 2, 3, (CT) 2, Sp 1, UK 7, 10, 11, US (NY) 1.

2. Regional Bibliographies

Regional bibliographies are those which cover the whole of Africa and all or most subjects (*a*) or single or limited groups of subjects (*b*), and those which cover a single region or country. In this group I include only those works published in the form of printed or reduplicated lists, reserving those which appear as cards or "fiches" for the next section. The figures on the right-hand side are the numbers of titles.

(a) All Africa, all subjects

Ang 1–3	14 × 3
Bel 2–2	1 500–2 000
Fr 3	*c.* 3 000
Sp 1	*c.* 500 but includes the Arab world
UK 1–1	*c.* 2 300 with the main emphasis on ethnology, sociology, and linguistics
UK 3	400 books in western European languages
UK 11	200 annotated book titles
UK (Ox) 1–1	300 articles from French, U.S. and British periodicals

(b) All Africa, limited subjects

Fr 6	Social sciences (sociology 87, political sciences 274, economics 325, anthropology 1 090 titles)
Bel Ter 1	Ethnology 2 158 titles
Fr 11	Economics, number not given but less than 1 080
Ug 2	Geography (East African section of *Bibl. geog. int.*, 150)
UK 5	Physical and social anthropology, archaeology, linguistics, *c.* 930
UK 4	Official publications, *c.* 7 000 from all Commonwealth countries and a law supplement
UK 6	Geography, 230 + 85 maps
US (NY) 2	Geography, 430
UK 7	Law, number unknown
UK (Ab 1)	Christian history of Africa
UK (Ab 3)	Modern African religious movements, began in 1968
US 3	Agriculture, *c.* 14 000 (subject headings)
Fr 10	Fruit, *c.* 6 000, but not solely relating to Africa

(c) African regions or countries, normally most subjects

Fr 2	French-speaking Africa, 650
Fr 4	French West Africa, mainly economics, 360
Mad 1	Madagascar, 2 788, joint national–regional
Nig (Ib) 1	Nigeria, 786, joint national–regional
Por 1	Portuguese Africa and neighbouring countries, 500
Tan 2	Tanzania, *c.* 500
Ug 1	Uganda, *c.* 580

As will be seen, no African regional bibliography covering all subjects contains more than 3 000 titles and only two annually contribute over 2 000, yet some current subject bibliographies list 1 500–2 000 titles and one, that for agriculture, claims to list about 14 000 "subject headings".

3. Regional Bibliographies Published as Cards or "Fiches"

The *Survey* lists nine of these, of which only two are produced outside France.

Bel 3-1	CIDESA. 15 000 annually on politics, economics and sociology
Fr 1-1	CARDAN. "Fiches analytiques", 1 800; "fiches signalétiques" 2 100; humanities and social sciences (sciences humaines)
Fr 1-2	CARDAN. "Fiches ouvrages", 1 618 in vol. 1, 4 133 in vol. 2
Fr 5	INSEE. 2 750 a year, last issue for 1966 had 106 on Africa
Fr 8	Bureau de recherches géologiques et minières, 105 in the May 1968 number
Fr 12-2	Bureau interafricain des sols, 900–1 000, soil
Fr 14-1	FNSP (Fiches de documentation africaine). 2 520 articles, 490 books, politics, sociology, economics
Fr 14-2	FNSP (Bibl. courante sur fiches d'articles de périodiques). 19 300 in 1966, politics, sociology, economics, of which 2 520 related to Africa. A cumulated set of volumes, comprising 304 000 "fiches" issued since 1946, was to be published in 1968.
UK (Ab) 2	Scottish Institute of Missionary Studies to make cards available to members in sets.

4. Abstracts and Analyses

Some services which provide more than the bare title and bibliographical reference have been mentioned in the previous section. Others appear in regular book or article format. Preeminent among them is the I.A.I.'s *African abstracts* (UK 1–2), for which a French version, *Analyses africaines* (Fr 1–3) has appeared since 1967. The *Survey* also records in this category:

Ang 1–2	Boletím analitico (Inst. de Angola)
Fr 9	Chronique des mines et de la recherche minière
Fr 12–1	Bulletin analytique mensuel (Bureau Interafricain des Sols)
Fr 14–4	Bulletin analytique de documentation économique et sociale contemporaine (FNSP)
Neth 1	Tropical abstracts
UK (Ox) 2	World agricultural economics and rural sociology abstracts
Zam 1	Annotated bibliography and index of the geology of Zambia

Of these, only two (Fr 12–1 and Zam 1) are concerned solely with Africa.

5. *Theses and Work in Progress*

Most ambitious of the four services recorded are the CIDESA *Bulletin d'information sur les recherches dans les sciences humaines concernant l'Afrique* (Bel 3–2), which lists work in progress in the UDC groups 3, 6, and parts of 9, and *Africa: a list of current social science research by private scholars and academic centers* (formerly *External research list ... Africa,* US 2), which in its issue for 1966 included 550 titles of work completed in 1965–6 and in progress by American (*sc.* United States) scholars and foreigners working in the USA.

Eth 1–3 registers current research on Ethiopia and the Horn from all over the world, while SA 2 is a quarterly report on bibliographical progress.

6. *Monographic Series of Bibliographies*

Ten of these are recorded from five countries:

Bel 1–2	Bibliographies générales et spécialisées (CDA Brussels)
3–3	Enquêtes bibliographiques (CEDESA)

Fr 13	Bibliographies hydrogéologiques (Cté interafr. et hydr.)
SA (CT) 2	Bibliographical series (Univ. Cape Town, School of Librarianship)
UK 1–4	Africa bibliography series (I.A.I.)
UK 10	Guides to materials for West African history in European archives (Univ. London, Inst. Hist. Research)
UK 13	Selected reading lists for advanced study (Cmw. Inst.)
US 1	Guides to government publications of sub-Saharan Africa (LC)
3–2	Occasional bibliography series (Syracuse U.)
US (NY) 3–1	Eastern African bibliography series (Syracuse U.)

7. Lists of Periodicals

Eth 1–2	List of current periodical publications in Ethiopia, published every two years since 1964
SA 1–3	Current South African periodicals—a classified list. Annual supplements list periodical births and deaths (and presumably marriages)
SA (CT) 1–2	Each issue of *Quarterly bulletin of the South African Library* contains a feature on 'South African periodical publications' which lists births, deaths, changes of name, with details of dates and subscriptions payable

8. Library Accessions Lists

Information is given about 13 lists of acquisitions taken in by libraries. Some of these are union lists: the Centre de documentation africaine in the Bibliothèque Albert Ier (formerly B. Royale), Bel 1, had some 30 000 titles in its *fichier* on 1 May 1967, but it does not publish any accessions lists; the Scandinavian Institute of African Studies (SCA 1) publishes a *Bulletin* three times a year of Africana additions to Scandinavian libraries. The *Joint Acquisitions List* published at Northwestern University, Evanston, U.S.A., in its bi-monthly bulletin published in March 1967 reproduced catalogue entries supplied by 17 co-operating institutions, some outside the United States.

The increase of the collections of individual libraries is

regularly announced by the following: Bibliothèque africaine (Bel 2–1) (about 1 000 titles a year), B. Musée de l'Homme (480), Padmore Research Library (230), Royal Library, Copenhagen (885 in two years), S.O.A.S. (2 271), Univ. of Dar-es-Salaam (*c.* 1 600 but not all Africana), and I.C.S. Oxford (1 500, ditto).

Some of the accessions lists include articles: thus Inst. de Angola (*c.* 1 200) and the Archives de Sénégal (1 400).[3]

9. *Miscellaneous*

Inevitably we finish up with a remnant consisting of bibliographical services of varying character not assignable to any of our former categories. Ger 2 is an entry for a quarterly review, *Mundus,* of German research contributions on Asia, Africa and Latin America, in which the titles of books and articles, and the comments on them are given in English for the benefit of those who cannot read German. A service starting in mid-1967 is recorded at Ger 3: the Deutsches Institut für Afrika-Forschung e. v. (Hamburg) proposed to supply "documentation (card service), bibliographies on special subjects, registers of Africa experts, etc.".

The *Bibliography of African bibliographies,* published every five to seven years by the South African Public Libraries, is entered at SA (CT) 1–3. The fourth edition (1961) contained about 1 340 titles. Also entered at SA (CT) 1–4 are details of the Mendelssohn Revision Project.

Nig (Ib) 2 is a bookseller's catalogue service; UK 8 the *British national bibliography.* Finally US (NY) is a bibliography on Africa south of the Sahara for undergraduate libraries, published in a preliminary edition in the fall of 1967 and in a final edition in the spring of 1969.

If, indeed, there is scope for the merger of existing services or even for the elimination of others, to increase and rationalize the potential for Africa bibliography, it is hoped that

---

[3] The I.A.I. adds approximately 2 000 titles every year to its classified card index. These titles also appear in the quarterly bibliography published in the Institute's journal *Africa,* which is available also in offprint form.

this categorization of the titles listed in the *Survey* will point to places where co-ordination of this kind might be promoted. In the tables which follow, I have tried to show how Africa is covered by bibliographical work, both regionally and subject-wise.

The *Survey* performs yet another useful function in giving figures for titles included in every service registered. While an uncountable amount of duplication of these must exist between the various bibliographies, nevertheless a totalling of the figures will give a maximum which will with some degree of clarity indicate the total world production of "Africana". This exercise in "bibliometrics" should be undertaken without excessive delay: it is an essential prerequisite for all discussion of the logistics or the establishment of an international African bibliographical and documentation centre.

Conspectus of Bibliographies Listed in the Survey

		1	2	3	4	5	6
Ang	1–1	*					
	1–2	*					Portuguese overseas territories
	1–3	*					
Bel	1–1		*				
	1–2		*				
	2–1		*				
	2–2		*				
	3–1		*			Economics, Politics, Sociology	
	3–2		*			UDC CDU classes 3, 6, 9 (parts)	
	3–3		*			Economics, Politics, Sociology	Especially former Belgian terrotories
(Ter)	1		*			Ethnology	Except Ethiopia, Madagascar
Eth	1–1			*			
	1–2			*			and publications of

		1	2	3	4	5	6
	1–3				*		E.C.A. and the Horn
Fr	1–1	*					
	1–2	*					
	1–3	*					
	2			*			French Africa excluding North
	3		*				
	4			*		Economics	French West
	5	*				Statistics, Economics	
	6	*				Social Sciences (Sociology, Politics, Economics, Anthropology)	
	7	*					
	8		*			Geology, Mining	
	9	*				Applied Geology	
	10	*				Fruit	
	11			*		Economics, Technology	French Africa and Madagascar
	12–1		*			Soil	
	12–2		*			Soil	
	13			*		Hydrology	French Africa
	14–1		*			Economics, Politics, Sociology	
	14–2	*				Economics, Politics, Sociology	
Fr	14–3	*				Economics, Politics, Sociology	
	14–4	*				Economics, Politics, Sociology	
Ger	1		*				
	2	*					
	3		*				

		1	2	3	4	5	6
Gh	1				*		
Mad	1				*		
Mal	1				*		
Neth	1	*				Tropical agriculture	
Nig(Ib)	1				*		
	2				*		
(Z)	1				*		Northern Nigeria
Por	1			*			Portuguese Africa
Rhod	1				*		
Sca	1		*				
	2		*			Social Sciences, Linguistics, Fiction	Main emphasis
SA	1-1	*			*		
	1-2	*			*		
	1-3	*					
	2			*			Southern
	3			*			Southern
(CT)	1-1				*		
	1-2				*		
	1-3		*				
	1-4			*			Southern
	2			*			Rhodesia & Southern
Sen	1				*		and French West
S.L.	1				*		
Sp	1		*				and Arab countries
Tan	1	*					
	2				*		
	3		*				East and Central
Ug	1				*		
	2			*		Geography	East
UK	1-1		*			Ethnology, Sociology, Linguistics	Main emphasis

	1	2	3	4	5	6
1–2		*			Ethnology, Sociology, Linguistics	Main emphasis
1–3		*				
1–4		*				
2		*				
3		*			Humanities	
4			*		Law Supplement	Commonwealth
5	*				Anthropology, Archaeology, Linguistics	
6	*				Geography	
7	*				Law	
8	*					
9	*					
10	*		*		History	West
11	*					
12	*				Aid, Development	
13	*		*			Commonwealth
14	*					
(Ab) 1		*			Christianity	
2	*				Missions	
UK(Ab) 3		*			Religious Movements	
(Ox) 1–1	*		*		Economics, Politics, Sociology	Commonwealth
1–2	*		*		Economics, Politics, Sociology	Commonwealth
2	*				Agriculture	
US 1		*				
2		*			Social Sciences	excluding South
3	*				Agriculture	
4		*				
(Ev) 1		*				

	1	2	3	4	5	6
(NY) 1		*				
2	*				Geography	
3–1			*			East & Southern
3–2						East & Southern
(St) 1	*					
Zam 1			*		Geology	

Col. 1 = Those services covering wider regions than Africa alone.
Col. 2 = All services which give their scope as Africa (including or excluding North Africa and Egypt), Black Africa (Afrique Noire), Africa South of the Sahara, Africa and Madagascar.
Col. 3 = Smaller regions of Africa, i.e. Francophone, Portuguese, Commonwealth, Southern.
Col. 4 = Single countries (including national bibliographies, which may, of course, include work about other African countries).
Col. 5 = Subject coverage as given by the respondents to the questionnaire, abbreviated where necessary. When no subject is given, the bibliography may include only humanities and social sciences or everything.
Col. 6 = Notes on the limitations of the area covered.

A most useful index to subjects reported as being covered by the various bibliographies was compiled by Miss Jenifer Cheetham, a student of librarianship, and is reproduced here, by permission. It does not embrace those works which are said to cover all subjects.

Subject index

Administration (7): Bel 2–1, Bel 2–2, Bel 3–2, UK 1–1, UK 1–2, UK 1–3, US 1.
Agriculture (10): Bel 2–1, Bel 2–2, Fr 3, Ger 1, Neth 1, UK 1–3, UK (Ox) 2, US 3, US 4, US (St) 1.
Anthropology (13): Fr 1–1, Fr 1–2, Fr 2, Fr 6, Fr 7, Ger 1, UK 1–1, UK 1–2, UK 1–3, UK 5, US 5, US (NY) 1, US (St) 1.
Archaeology (12): Bel (Ter), Fr 1–1, Fr 1–2, Fr 2, Fr 3, Fr 7, UK 1–1,

UK 1–2, UK 1–3, UK 5, US (NY) 1, US (St) 1.

Arts (12): Bel 2–1, Bel 2–2, Bel (Ter), Fr 3, Ger 1, Ger 2, UK 1–1, UK 1–2, UK 1–3, US 4, US (NY) 1, US (St) 1.

Cosmology (3): UK 1–1, UK 1–2, UK 1–3.

Economics (19): Bel 2–1, Bel 2–2, Bel 3–1, Bel 3–2, Bel 3–3, Bel (Ter), Fr 1–1, Fr 1–2, Fr 2, Fr 3, Fr 4, Fr 5, Fr 6, Ger 1, UK 1–1, UK 1–2, UK 1–3, US 2, US 4, US (NY)1.

Education (15): Bel 2–1, Bel 2–2, Bel 3–1, Bel 3–2, Bel (Ter), Fr 2, Fr 3, Ger 1, UK 1–1, UK 1–2, UK 1–3, US 2, US 4, US (NY) 1, US (St) 1.

Ethnography (12): Bel 2–1, Bel 2–2, Bel (Ter), Fr 2, Fr 3, Fr 7, Ger 1, UK 1–1, UK 1–2, UK 1–3, UK 1–4, UK 5.

Folklore (5): Fr 7, UK 1–1, UK 1–2, UK 1–3, US 4.

Fruit Research (1): Fr 10.

Geography (12): Bel 2–1, Bel 2–2, Fr 2, Fr 3, Fr 7, Ger 1, US 2, UK 6, US 2, US 4, US (NY) 1, US (St) 1.

Geology (3): Fr 7, Fr 8, Fr 9.

Government (8): Bel 3–2, UK 1–1, UK 1–2, UK 1–3, US 2, US 4, US (NY) 1, US (St) 1.

Health (6): Fr 2, UK 1–1, UK 1–2, UK 1–3, US 4, US (St) 1.

History (15): Bel 2–1, Bel 2–2, Bel (Ter), Fr 1–1, Fr 1–2, Fr 2, Fr 3, Ger 1, UK 1–1, UK 1–2, UK 1–3, UK 10, US 2, US 4, US (NY) 1, US (St) 1, UK (Ab) 3, UK (Ab) 1.

Language & Linguistics (13): Bel 2–1, Bel 2–2, Bel (Ter), Fr 1–1, Fr 1–2, Fr 2, Fr 3, Fr 7, Ger 1, UK 1–1, UK 1–2, UK 1–3, UK 1–4, UK 5, US 2, US 4, US (NY) 1, US (St) 1.

Law (12): Bel 2–1, Bel 2–2, Fr 2, Fr 3, Ger 1, UK 1–1, UK 1–2, UK 1–3, UK 7, US 2, US 4, US (St) 1.

Literature (12): Bel 2–1, Bel 2–2, Fr 3, Ger 1, UK 1–1, UK 1–2, UK 1–3, UK 1–4, US 2, US 4, US (NY) 1, US (St) 1.

Medicine (8): Bel 2–1, Bel 2–2, Ger 1, UK 1–1, UK 1–2, UK 1–3, US 4, US (St) 1.

Missions (5): Bel 2–1, Bel 2–2, Fr 2, UK (Ab) 2, US (St) 1.

Nutrition (4): UK 1–1, UK 1–2, UK 1–3, US 3.

Philosophy (6): Ger 1, UK 1–1, UK 1–2, UK 1–3, US 2, US (NY) 1.

Politics (16): Bel 2–1, Bel 2–2, Bel (Ter), Fr 1–1, Fr 1–2, Fr 2, Fr 3, Fr 6, Ger 1, UK 1–1, UK 1–2, UK 1–3, US 2, US 4, US (NY) 1. US (St) 1.

Religion (13): Bel 2–1, Bel 2–2, Fr 2, Fr 3, Ger 1, UK 1–1, UK 1–2, UK 1–3, UK (Ab) 2, US 2, US 4, US (NY) 1, US (St) 1.

Sociology (15): Bel 2–1, Bel 2–2, Bel 3–3, Bel (Ter), Fr 1–1, Fr 1–2, Fr 2, Fr 3, Fr 6, Fr 7, Ger 1, UK 1–1, UK 1–2, UK 1–3, US (NY) 1, US (St) 1.

Soil (1): Fr. 12–1.
Witchcraft (3): UK 1–1, UK 1–2, UK 1–3.

The number of bibliographies for each subject is given in parentheses.

It seems clear that bibliographies compiled from a discipline approach tend to contain much material missed by those starting from a regional one, in that the two compilers tend to search different periodicals, with a comparatively small overlap. This is also true of an Africanist *vis-à-vis* a Commonwealth approach, as was shown by Mr. J. S. T. Thompson, who made a numerical comparison of titles included in the "Bibliography of current publications" in *Africa* and the *List of periodical articles* published by the Oxford Institute of Commonwealth Studies.[4]

Developments since the Nairobi Conference

It may fairly be claimed that the Conference represented a landmark in the history of African bibliography. In sessions allocated to the study and discussion of national or country bibliographies, subject bibliographies, current bibliography and automation, classification and cataloguing, bibliographical control of special types of material (government publications, work in progress, manuscripts and archives, microfilms, ephemeral materials, and sound recordings), acquisition of African materials and the international co-ordination of bibliographical services, the deliberations of the Conference amount to a survey of the "state of the art" or an *où en est la bibliographie africaine*.

Through its recommendations, sent to all Ministers of Education in tropical African countries and other organizations capable of implementing them, the Conference sought to indicate approaches which would benefit the process of recording

[4] It seems that 169 relevant articles about Africa included in the Oxford list covering the period October 1966 to December 1966 were not to be found in the I.A.I. Bibliography.

sources of information on Africa. The present section of this paper seeks to report, at a distance of two years since "Nairobi", solely developments which have occurred and measures which are being taken which, though in the spirit of the Nairobi recommendations, may not be directly attributable to them, and are, in fact, *post hoc* but not necessarily *propter hoc*. It does not attempt to record all African bibliographical work undertaken or published since December 1967.

In preparing it, I must acknowledge the great assistance provided by many persons, but especially by Ruth Jones and the librarians who attended a discussion of developments since "Nairobi" at the Commonwealth Africa University Libraries Conference held at Lusaka in 1969.

The value of conferences such as these does not lie only in the stimulus given to the compilation of useful papers and other documents nor in the opportunity provided for the exchange of information and discussion by practitioners of different nations, but also in the facilities afforded for these persons to meet their foreign colleagues, to make original contacts and to develop and renew those made on earlier occasions. It would be quite impossible to estimate the number of fringe benefits which accrued as a result of the presence in Nairobi at the same time of experts from so many countries. One event planned by the organisers of the conference was a meeting of several members of the Standing Conference of African University Libraries (SCAUL), who had been able to come together for the first time since the Leverhulme Conference of 1965. Another was that the editor of a definitive Belgian Congo bibliography was able to enlist on the spot collaborators for the Rwanda and Burundi sections of his work. A third was that plans were made for a German delegate to supply entries for German-language publications on Tanzania and Uganda to the compiler of the current bibliographies for those countries and this he has continued to do ever since the Conference.

In the remaining paragraphs of this article I shall attempt to record the developments in African bibliography which have occurred since the Nairobi Conference, in the first instance relating these to the resolutions which were passed by the members of the Conference and which are here reprinted for the sake of convenience.

Promotion of African national bibliographies

1. That African governments should promote, as a matter of urgency, the compilation of national bibliographies listing all current material published in each country.
2. That financial assistance should be given to African libraries to enable them to search for, collect, and record non-current material. This assistance might take the form of (*a*) the provision of photographic equipment, particularly portable microfilm cameras, and (*b*) personnel competent to use this equipment and versed in bibliographic techniques.
3. That African bibliographic and acquisitions projects should include within their scope locally published ephemeral materials, such as political-party and trade-union documents, "market literature", conference papers, and mimeographed reports, which are essential for research.

Although subsumed under the heading of "Promotion of African national bibliographies", resolutions 2 and 3 would appear to have little to do with this topic, and resolution 3, which relates really to questions of book acquisitions, might more properly have been placed with resolution 16.

The University Libraries in Uganda (as already reported at the Conference itself by Mr. Lwanga, see *Report*, p. 299), Kenya and Zambia have followed Tanzania's example by incorporating in their respective accessions lists or gazettes the titles of books and pamphlets published in those countries and obtained by the libraries.

The UNESCO has awarded a contract to the Library School at Dakar University for the compilation and publication of a national bibliography for 1967 of French-speaking countries in Africa. This will be compiled by Mr. Bousso, with the assistance of former students of the School. Another contract for a similar bibliography of anglophone West Africa has been awarded to Mr. Kotei.

In Ethiopia the Research and Curriculum Library of the Ministry of Education has distributed to research workers and education experts a cyclostyled list of *Educational publications and documentation.*

Bibliographies promulgated by the National Library of Nigeria include *Index to selected Nigerian publications* (1965), *Religious literature in the vernacular in the National Library* (NLP 7), *A bibliography of biographies and memoirs on Nigeria* (NLP9), and *Books on Nigerian languages: a bibliography* (NLP 10).

A circular was submitted to librarians in Kenya, Tanzania and Uganda by Prof. Langlands proposing a combined national bibliography for the three countries. The Professor now regularly receives from Dr. Scholz cards with titles of German writings on Tanzania or Uganda for his bibliographies of the two countries.

One matter may be reported under resolution 2. A group of German librarians, at the suggestion of Dr. Scholz, has arranged for the presentation of theses submitted to German universities to national libraries in African countries.

Legal deposit

4. That, because material printed in Africa is difficult to locate, owing to the fact that the publishing and bookselling trades are under-developed, African governments should enact publication deposit laws (where these are not already in force) and, where desirable, place the responsibility for deposit on printers rather than publishers.

5. That scholars and others undertaking research in Africa should be required to deposit the results of that research with the national library and/or archives of the country in question.

Uganda and Nigeria are now placing the onus of legal deposit on printers in those countries.

The Inaugural Conference to discuss Co-operation among Universities in Eastern Africa, held at Addis Ababa in December 1968, recommended the recognition, by law, of university libraries as the official repositories for government and all other publications in the country concerned. This recommendation was reiterated by the Lusaka Conference.

The Library of the University of Zambia has been designated as the National Reference Library for the country, but awaits legislation conferring upon it the right to demand legal deposit.

The Lusaka Conference echoed the provisions of resolution 5 (in its resolution IX, i, ii, and iii) and declared that procedures and regulations applied in granting approval for research projects should be widely publicized. Further that registers of research should be published where these do not exist already, and that, inevitably, a *register registrorum* should be compiled.

Bibliographical training in Africa

6. That, because of the obvious advantages gained from meetings between English- and French-speaking specialists, as demonstrated at the Nairobi Conference, occasional meetings should be held of those responsible for professional training in schools of librarianship in Africa for the purpose of planning (*a*) curricula and methods of teaching with particular reference to the teaching of bibliography, and (*b*) the provision of introductory courses in bibliographical research for both library students and university students in general.

So far as is known, this suggestion, resulting from a proposal by M. Amadou Bousso (*Report,* Appendix, p. 322) has not as yet been taken up by any organization.

On training in general there are several developments to report. A six-week course on documentation, conducted by the Friedrich Naumann-Stiftung on behalf of the UNESCO has been held at the East African School of Librarianship at Makerere University. The ASLIB is hoping to arrange short courses of training in librarianship and technical information work in selected African countries. The School of Library, Archive and Information Studies at University College, London, has established a new course designed to give the relevant training necessary for modern archivists working in developing countries and elsewhere.

The Lusaka Conference believed that the general education, enlightenment and broadening of experience of middle-level and senior staff should be supported, in addition to formal library training. Instructions should consider a variety of programmes to accomplish this, including local, regional and international work experience and travel at all levels (resolution X). It further noted with satisfaction that the East African Vice-Chancellors' meeting in Addis Ababa had stressed the importance of meetings and conferences of representatives from the various universities, and had included library science and "reprography" among subjects suitable for discussion at such gatherings.

The Inter-University Council for Higher Education Overseas, through its Manpower and Training Committee, set up a Working Party to study all aspects of training for librarianship overseas. In its report, soon to be submitted to the Council, proposals are made which, if accepted, will lead to great improvements in the facilities and opportunities offered for training in library schools, both abroad and in this country.

Finally, the SCOLMA has organized, since the Nairobi Conference, seminars held at the Royal Commonwealth Society, which have been addressed by British Africanists, African librarians, the Keeper of Public Archives, library-school teachers and students, and librarians in charge of African collections in Britain.

Classification and cataloguing of African material

7. That a group of specialists should be formed to promote and co-ordinate work on problems of African classification and cataloguing.

8. That M. Fontvieille's paper on the cataloguing of African names should be made available in an English version for the benefit of those concerned with similar problems in anglophone Africa.

The group of specialists has not yet been formed and M. Fontvieille's paper is not yet available in an English version. It was published in *Bulletin des bibliothèques de France* and will be re-published, with an English summary, in *The Bibliography of Africa* (1970).

These questions, again inevitably, came up for discussion at the Lusaka Conference, where a paper entitled "Classification and cataloguing of Africana", submitted by Wilfred J. Plumbe, modestly claimed to be no more than "an attempt to assemble in one document the existing references and data". Mr. Plumbe nevertheless set out what he thought to be the necessary action to be followed in respect of these twin problems and the Conference supported him to the extent of passing a series of resolutions aimed at (1) the adoption in each African country of the procedure followed in Senegal, whereby each author is required by legal decree to indicate on a title-page that part of his name under which he should be entered in catalogues, and (2) the compilation of definitive schedules for the classification of African history, languages and ethnology, of an authoritive list of entry headings for African authors and public figures, and of a list of the recommended names of African tribes and languages, a task already being undertaken by CARDAN. Furthermore, the Conference recommended that librarians in each African country should provide in their accessions lists schedules of the names of authors and local dignitaries, showing the preferred forms for catalogue entry of these names.

Archives

9. That African governments, recognising that archives are an invaluable source of research material, should ensure that their archives (both official and private) are (*a*) located in one place in proximity to a centre of learning, such as a university, (*b*) preserved and processed for use, (*c*) put in the charge of a qualified archivist, (*d*) housed in a building specially constructed for this purpose, and that systematic lists of these archives are compiled.

10. That funds should be sought to speed up the training of African archivists.

11. That an expanded and updated version of Baxter's *Archival facilities in sub-Saharan Africa* should be published, giving detailed descriptions of available finding aids and archival manuscript collections and an outline of work in progress or planned. That means should be sought for producing an annual account of work on archives and manuscript collections concerned with Africa.

12. That the International Council on Archives (I.C.A.) should be encouraged in its work of persuading all European

countries to produce inventories of their African material, where not satisfactorily completed already.

13. That all former colonial powers should be encouraged to form projects for the collection of private colonial archives similar to the Oxford Colonial Records Project, and to produce finding aids for such records.

14. That scholarly associations in Europe and the United States should encourage holders of African archival material to make microfilm copies available for deposit in suitable libraries or archives in Africa.

Some of these resolutions on archives merely represent a jumping on the band-waggon on the part of the Conference, as the action proposed was already in hand. One product, however, may be regarded as a direct result of the Conference: Louis Frewer's *Catalogue of African manuscripts in Rhodes House Library* is immediately attributable to an idea which germinated in the author's mind during his sojourn in Nairobi. Frewer was also the instigator of resolution 13: somewhat to their surprise, our German colleagues found on return to their country that preliminary soundings seemed to indicate that systematic searching for African materials still in private ownership would repay any effort put into it.

The International Council on Archives has been active in the promotion of African archival resources. An East African regional branch (EARBICA) has been formed, with headquarters in Nairobi, under the chairmanship of the National Archivist of Kenya. Surveys, leading to the supersession of Baxter's *Archival facilities,* have been made by Jeffrey Ede in East and Central Africa, by Morris Rieger in English-speaking West Africa, by Charles Kecskeméti in francophone West Africa and by Giovanni Antonelli in the Arab countries. Several guides for Africa in the UNESCO/ICA sponsored series "Sources for the history of the nations" have been completed and will be published this year. The British volume, compiled by Noel Matthews and M. Doreen Wainwright, has been passed for publication by the Oxford University Press on behalf of the S.O.A.S. It is also being used as a quarry for the British volume in the series of handy paperback booklets "Materials for the history of West Africa" being edited by the Institute of Historical Research in the University of London, in which several volumes for materials in other European countries have recently appeared, and others are in preparation.

For the training of archivists no funds have as yet been found, to my knowledge, but, as stated above, the School of Library, Archive and Information Science at University College, London, has devised a course specially designed to meet the needs of archivists from Africa, Asia and developing countries in other continents.

Importation of reading materials into African countries

15. That African governments should be urged to facilitate the entry of reading materials by exempting these from import taxes, in order to promote education and development in Africa.

Nothing to report.

Acquisition by libraries of materials produced in Africa

16. That the Library of Congress should seek to amend existing legislation so that it may be permitted to authorise its offices in Nairobi and elsewhere in Africa to collect African material for other libraries in the United States, as well as in Africa and other parts of the world.

This is another "band-waggon" resolution. The Library of Congress is now able to avail itself of authorizing legislation for the purchase of books by its Nairobi acquisitions office, but only for libraries in the United States, and for the present it lacks the funds necessary to give effect to this authorization. The Nairobi library, meanwhile, continues to collect publications over a wide tract of eastern Africa and to publish its most useful accessions lists. The Library of the S.O.A.S. has undertaken to provide cataloguing data for publications in certain African languages with which neither the Library of Congress nor its Nairobi office are able to cope, but there remain a small minority in languages too exotic even for the S.O.A.S.!

The SCOLMA devoted the larger part of its annual meeting, held in Birmingham in 1969, to the discussion of acquisition problems in collecting materials from Africa, with reports from many of the libraries participating in the area specialization scheme. The proceedings of the meeting have been published by the International Documentation Company of Zug, Switzerland, in a volume entitled *Conference on the acquisition of material from Africa, University of Birmingham, 25th April 1969*. Reports and papers compiled by Valerie Bloomfield, Zug (1969).

An article by Ernst Kohl published in 1969[5] dealt with the problem of acquisition of materials in Africa, the present state and plans for the solution of it. He made a detailed study of the current production of printers and publishers in Dahomey and Sierra Leone, and proposed measures which, though costly in themselves, represent a considerable saving over the cost of sending scholars to these countries to consult the local materials. He has followed up this study with an exhaustive inventory of the Dahomean periodical press.[6]

International co-ordination of bibliographical data

17. That an international network for the co-ordination of bibliographical data on Africa should be established. That a documentation centre provided with key-punching and computer equipment should be set up as soon as possible at a suitable location in Africa to form a link between (*a*) national and regional centres in Africa and (*b*) centres in other countries. That two international working parties, each consisting of five members (with power to co-opt to fill vacancies), should consider (1) the planning of the African centre and its connections with the other centres and (2) the standardization of methods and the compilation of a common bibliographical style and annotation scheme based, at least initially, on work in progress at Human Relations Area Files, Yale University.

18. That the UNESCO should be asked to consider sending, for the next few years, free copies of the *International biblio-*

---

[5] Zur Frage des Literaturerwerbs in Afrika: gegenwärtiger Stand und Möglichkeiten der Verbesserung. Ernst Kohl. Sonderbeilage zur Zeitschrift *Afrika heute*, Nr. 5/69, 1 März 1969.

[6] Bibliographie der Zeitschriften aus Dahomey. Zusammengestellt von Ernst Kohl. *Id.*, Nr 1/70, 15 Jan. 1970.

graphy of the social sciences, published annually in four parts by the Comité international pour la documentation des sciences sociales (CIDSS, Paris), at the request of UNESCO, to a centre in each country in Africa that would agree to send regularly to CIDSS classified and/or annotated lists of recent publications in the social sciences issued in that country, and that the national authority should provide the centre with financial assistance for this end, where needed. This exchange would serve two purposes: (*a*) ensuring that African publications are well represented in these international bibliographies, and (*b*) familiarizing researchers in Africa with publications which do not concern Africa but are useful to their work from a general, methodological or comparative point of view.

19. That an enquiry into sources of information on research in progress should be undertaken with a view to the co-ordination and avoidance of duplication of the work already being done by the Centre international de documentation économique et sociale africaine (CIDESA, Bruxelles) in connection with its *Bulletin of information on current research on human sciences concerning Africa.*

Perhaps the most far-reaching plans for the future are enshrined in the three resolutions passed on the subject of the international co-ordination of bibliographical data, especially the first, which I will leave to the last, as there is more, though not very substantial, progress to report. I do not know if the UNESCO has considered supplying to African countries complimentary copies of the *International bibliography of the social sciences,* nor do I know if the proposed enquiry into sources of information on research in progress has been set in motion, but on this topic I remind my readers of developments reported under Resolution 5.

The UNESCO is said to be considering summoning a meeting of experts to consider the need for and means of establishing a bibliographical centre in Africa along the lines of resolution 17. John Webster contributed a paper entitled "Toward an international automated bibliographic system for Africana" to panel IIIF (Research tools and the scholar) at the 11th annual meeting of the African Studies Association at Los Angeles in October 1968. Miriam Alman is working on a thesis devoted to this topic, which she hopes to submit for the degree of PH.D. in the University of London.

Before we can run, we must learn to walk, and it behoves us first to describe moves being made towards the co-ordination on the international plane of established hand-made bibliographies. Discussion took place at Nairobi about the possibility of issuing jointly under a single cover three current national bibliographies of Africa publications issued outside Africa, *United Kingdom publications and theses on Africa*, *United States and Canadian publications on Africa*, and the *Afrika-Bibliographie*. Before any sort of merger between these three guides can take place, it is obviously necessary that there should be tripartite agreement on questions of lay-out and arrangement and on the categorization of the material by subject and area. Work is proceeding on this and a measure of agreement has been reached, but progress is slow because of the seemingly intractable difficulties of speedy international communication. A fourth annual bibliography of this kind has just appeared: it is compiled by a consortium of French libraries known as CIDA (Centre interbibliothécaire de documentation africaine) and is published by CARDAN. This new entrant to the field has also agreed in principle to conform to any system subscribed to by the other three. A small but perhaps not unimportant achievement is hereby chronicled, for, if other countries will agree to compile similar regular bibliographies of their Africana production and will also agree to arrange these according to the rubrics selected by the others, one can conceive of an international centre supplied with, and making use of, an international documentation as nearly exhaustive as may be.

Neither of the two proposed international working parties has been able to secure the funds necessary to enable its members to meet. Three European members of the first did, however, contrive to come together in Paris in June 1969, with the Conference Secretary, and agreed to work along the lines suggested in the previous paragraph, but the *procès-verbal* of the meeting is still awaited, letters remain unanswered, and no further progress has been made. The second, concerned with the standardization of methods and the compilation of a common bibliographical style and annotation scheme based, at least initially, on work in progress at Human Relations Area Files, Yale University, has achieved much by means of an active correspondence and this progress has been described by John Webster in his paper. Two automated systems, HABS, the Yale Scheme, and ISIS, used by the Central Library and Documentation Branch of the International Labour Office in Geneva, are rival candidates, it seems, for the favours of the Working Party and until one of them is chosen as the more acceptable by all members, further advances are restricted. Lists of descriptors or agreed subject headings, to be used by all suppliers of information to the proposed international centre, are the subject of much discussion and hard work on the part of bodies of documentalists over much of the more developed world, and these lists, or a combination of them, constitute one of the essential prerequisites for the bringing into being of an international documentation centre for Africa. There will also be a great deal to do by way of systems analysis, design of programmes and planning of a complex multi-national organization before the Centre will be able to open its doors.

Conference reports and papers

20. That the possibility of publishing the proceedings and papers of the Conference should be explored, if this should seem desirable, in addition to the report which the International African Institute will publish in *Africa* and issue as an offprint.

21. Failing publication of the papers in full, that consideration should be given to the possibility of issuing further copies, whether in duplicated form or in print, for free distribution or for sale.

22. That high priority should be given to reproducing the *Survey of current bibliographical services*.

It did seem desirable and arrangements were made for the publication of the proceedings and papers in the spring of 1970 by Frank Cass Ltd. The volume has been edited by the Conference Chairman and Secretary. It will include the *Survey of current bibliographical services*.

Future meetings

23. That the International Conference on African Bibliography should meet periodically, possibly immediately before the meetings of the International Congress of Africanists, and the International African Institute should continue to serve as its secretariat.

No plans exist at present for a second meeting of the International Conference on African Bibliography, but all possibilities will be energetically explored.

From all of what has been said, it would seem that the Conference has acted as a powerful stimulus to bibliographical work on Africa, even if it did not immediately originate it. The remark made at the opening dinner that "Nairobi" would be regarded as a watershed in African bibliography seems to have been fully justified.

Contributors

N. O. Arunsi is Acquisitions Librarian at the University of Dar es Salaam since July, 1969. He recieved his B.A. and his Post Graduate Diploma in Librarianship from the Universities of Nigeria and Ibadan in 1963 and 1964. In 1964 he was Assistant Librarian at the University of Ibadan and joined the staff of the University of Nigeria, Nsukka as Sub-Librarian in 1965. He underwent special training in Comparative Librarianship in 1966–67.

S. W. Hockey is Director of the Swaziland National Library Service since 1970. He was trained at the University College School of Librarianship in London 1930–33. 1934–48 he worked in English County Libraries. He was Director of the Eastern Caribbean Regional Library 1948–53, of the Jamaica Library Service 1953–55, and of the Trinidad Central Library and Eastern Caribbean Regional Library 1956–60. During 1962–64 he was Libraries Organizer in East Africa and during 1960–69 he was Director of the East African Literature Bureau.

I. M. N. Kigongo-Bukenya is in charge of the Processing Department at the Public Libraries Board Headquarters in Kampala. He was educated at Makerere College School and was later trained and qualified as a teacher at Namutamba College. He graduated from the East African School of Librarianship at Makerere University in 1969. As part of his Diploma in Librarianship he wrote a thesis on "Development of Public Libraries in Uganda".

T. K. Lwanga is University Librarian at Makerere University since 1968. He graduated from the School of Librarianship at Loughborough College of Further Education and took his B.Sc. at the University of London. He has been Senior Library Assistant at Croydon Public Libraries and Library Assistant, Assistant Librarian, and Deputy Librarian at Makerere University.

P. J. Mhaiki is Director of the Institute of Adult Education at the University of Dar-es-Salaam since 1970. He took his B.A. at Duquesne University. He has taught and administered in the secondary schools in Tanzania during the years 1959–68. He was appointed Regional Education Officer of Iringa region in 1969, Assistant Director of National Education and National Director UNDP/UNESCO Functional Adult Literacy Project the same year.

J. Ndegwa, A.L.A., F.L.A., has been the University Librarian of the University of Nairobi since 1967. He was Librarian at the East African Literature Bureau from 1958 to 1963. He was Assistant Librarian at University College, Nairobi, from 1958 to 1963 and Deputy Librarian in 1965–66.

T. Nilsson is Trade Unionist and Adult Educator within the Swedish Labour Movement. He has studied Socio-Economics and Politics in Europe, the USA and East Africa. He has been Tutor Adult Education Trainer at the Institute of Adult Education, University of Dar-es-Salaam 1968–70. He is Consultant to the Swedish International Development Authority since 1965.

T. O. Pala is Chief Librarian of the Kenya National Library Service. He took his B.A. at London University and his M.A. at Columbia University, New York. He received his B.L.S. (Bachelor of Library) degree from McGill University. He has been Librarian at the Institute of Education at Makerere University and Assistant Librarian at the University of Nairobi.

J. D. Pearson is the Librarian of the School of Oriental and African Studies at the University of London since 1950. He entered service of the University Library in Cambridge in 1928, Rogerson Hebrew Scholar at St. John's College in Cambridge 1932–36, Browne Memorial Student at Pembroke College in Cambridge 1936–38. He was in charge of the Oriental Department at the Cambridge University Library 1938–39 and 1946–49.

Rede Perry-Widstrand was educated at the University of Saskatchewan and received her library-science degree at McGill University. She has worked in various public libraries in Canada and was the Librarian of the Institute of Adult Education, University College, Dar-es-Salaam, from 1965 to 1967. She is now Associate Librarian at the Dag Hammarskjöld Library of International Affairs at Uppsala.

S. S. Saith is Director of the East African School of Librarianship at Makerere University since 1968. He took his B.Sc. at Punjab University 1929 and his M.A. at Edinburgh 1932. He received his University Diploma in Librarianship from London University 1934 and his F.L.A. 1941. He was University Librarian 1941–48 at Punjab University. Librarian at the Ministry of External Affairs in New Dehli 1949-60, Honorary Director and Director of the Institute of Librarianship at the University of New Delhi 1951–63. During 1963–67 he was a UNESCO Expert in Librarianship at he Advanced Teacher Training College, Owerri, Nigeria and 1967–68 he was Unesco Library Consultant at the National Library of Nigeria in Lagos.

A.-B. Wallenius is the Librarian of the Scandinavian Institute of African Studies in Uppsala since 1970. She took her B.A. at the University of Uppsala in 1943 and graduated from the Swedish School of Librarianship in Stockholm in 1957. She entered service of the University Library in Uppsala the same year. In 1965–69 she was Assistant Librarian and Acting Librarian at the Scandinavian Institute of African Studies in Uppsala.

M. C. G. Wise, F.L.A., has been Sub-Librarian at the College of Librarianship, Aberystwyth, Wales, since 1969. He was Assistant Librarian in the reference service of Kensington Public Library in London from 1953 to 1957 and at the Royal Technical College/Royal College in Nairobi from 1957 to 1961. During the period 1962–69 he was Assistant Librarian/Deputy Librarian at the University College in Dar-es-Salaam. He has been examiner to the East African School of Librarianship at Makerere University College.

Z
851
E3
L5

OCT 26 1972